P9-AOE-321

Criminal Justice
Recent Scholarship

Edited by
Marilyn McShane and Frank P. Williams III

A Series from LFB Scholarly

DISCARD
Property of WLU
Social Work Library

Violent and Non-Violent Disputes Involving Gang Youth

Lorine A. Hughes

LFB Scholarly Publishing LLC
New York 2005

Copyright © 2005 by LFB Scholarly Publishing LLC

All rights reserved.

Library of Congress Cataloging-in-Publication Data

Hughes, Lorine A., 1974-
  Violent and non-violent : disputes involving gang youth / Lorine A.
Hughes.
      p. cm. -- (Criminal justice (LFB Scholarly Publishing LLC))
  Includes bibliographical references and index.
  ISBN 1-59332-098-1 (alk. paper)
  1. Gangs--Illinois--Chicago Metropolitan Area. 2. Violence in
adolescence--Illinois--Chicago Metropolitan Area. 3. Violent crimes--
Illinois--Chicago Metropolitan Area. 4. Chicago Metropolitan Area
(Ill.)--Social conditions. I. Title. II. Series.
  HV6439.U7I4546 2005
  364.1'066'097731--dc22

2005021182

ISBN 1-59332-098-1

Printed on acid-free 250-year-life paper.

Manufactured in the United States of America.

Table of Contents

List of Tables

Introduction

In the latter half of the 20th century, we have witnessed a rapid proliferation of adolescent street gangs and the emergence of a few "super gangs" in some of the nation's largest cities (Klein 1995). Simultaneously glamorized and demonized in the media and dubbed a menace to society by law enforcement and other agents of social control, these seemingly hostile groups of youth have been the source of much public fascination and concern. They have also received considerable research attention, as evidenced by the substantial scholarly literature that now exists on the topic.

Although there has been a virtual explosion of information concerning the distribution and composition of gangs, the background characteristics of individual gang members, and various approaches to gang control (see Coughlin and Venkatesh 2003; Esbensen et al. 2004; Huff 2002; Hughes 2005; Klein et al. 1995; Short and Hughes forthcoming; Spergel 1995), understanding of the behavior of gangs and their members is still elusive. A major reason for the lack of progress in this area is that "microsocial phenomena have been largely ignored" (Short 1998:19). Indeed, most gang studies reflect larger criminological trends in that they focus mainly on macrosocial or individual levels of explanation, to the general neglect of those interaction processes and situational characteristics that may account for the well-documented gang "facilitative" effect.[1]

---

[1] Longitudinal analyses of self-report data indicate that delinquent behavior increases during periods of active gang membership, compared to periods before and after (see, e.g., Thornberry et al. 1993, 2003). Such findings

1

Students of violence traditionally have paid only scant attention to the behavioral effects of microsocial phenomena. Recently, however, a handful of scholars have begun to examine the sequence of events and behaviors that transpire during the course of violent encounters, focusing in particular on (1) offender and victim behaviors related to the maintenance of socially acceptable situated identities and (2) the general influence of more tangible situational characteristics, such as the setting, third parties, intoxicants, and weapons. Although such studies have made important contributions to the literature, understanding of the causal effects of microsocial phenomena has been precluded by the dearth of empirical data and theoretical guidance concerning "non-incidents"—more particularly, non-violent incidents (Sampson and Lauritsen 1994). In most studies, data are obtained from official homicide or assault records or by asking incarcerated individuals about the violent incident(s) that led to their current state of lock-up (but see Wells and Horney 2002). Treating the officially defined violent incident as the unit of analysis, researchers then attempt to determine the proportion of incidents in which identities are attacked, third parties are present and intervene, the victim resists, participants are intoxicated, and so on. This type of descriptive work clearly is a useful first step, but "[i]f research is to move beyond description, researchers must be interested as much in situations that do not produce deviance as those that do" (Birbeck and LaFree 1993:122-123).

Under the risk-factor prevention paradigm outlined by Farrington (2000; see also Farrington 1998), microsocial phenomena can be conceptualized as both potential risks and potential protectors. A pressing task for criminologists is to determine the circumstances associated with each of these possibilities. Confronting this intellectual challenge will require methodological adjustments, however. While sampling on the dependent variable is sometimes necessary, adoption of more inclusive sampling strategies will facilitate comparisons across incidents with a variety of outcomes. Such comparisons are needed if we are to understand the etiological significance of microsocial contexts.

---

strongly suggest that there is something about gangs themselves that facilitates or causes the bad behavior of their members.

Using field observations made by youth gang workers and others (e.g., graduate students) who were associated with the Program for Detached Workers of YMCA of Metropolitan Chicago or with the University of Chicago between 1959 and 1962 (see Short and Strodtbeck 1965), the research reported in this book examines the influence of interaction processes and situational characteristics on both violent and non-violent dispute-related incidents. Chapter 1 provides a detailed review of the treatment of microsocial phenomena in extant criminological literature and traces the development of relevant theoretical perspectives. The major situational correlates of crime and violence are identified and reviewed in chapter 2. In chapter 3, I focus specifically on gang research and discuss the importance of the microsocial level of explanation in that body of work. A total of 13 hypotheses are derived from impression management theory and presented in chapter 4. Each of these hypotheses involves predictions about the importance of one of several microsocial variables suggested by the literature as relevant to the occurrence of violence. Data and methods are described in Chapter 5, as is the missing data problem. In chapter 6, I present findings from quantitative analyses of the data. Although Hughes and Short (2005) have used multivariate models to examine these data, the current study focuses on univariate and bivariate analyses. When possible, interaction sequences are also examined. Results of each of these analyses generally are supportive of impression management theory in that disputes frequently are shown to unfold in a manner consistent with what we would expect given the immediate contexts and their impression (status) management implications. Chapter 7 presents findings from qualitative analyses of the narrative data. These analyses are oriented toward theoretical elaboration, with emphasis on themes related to the conditions under which disputes are likely to emerge in the social milieu of gangs and either escalate into violence or be "squashed." In Chapter 8, I conclude the study by summarizing key findings, discussing potential limitations, and offering a few recommendations for future research.

CHAPTER 1

The Microsocial Level of Explanation

INTRODUCTION

Three different types of questions can be asked about violence (and other types of deviant activities), with answers to each making important but distinct contributions to our overall understanding of the phenomenon (Reiss and Roth 1993; Sampson and Lauritsen 1994). First, scholars can inquire as to why a specific individual (or individuals) engages in violent behavior. This level is herein referred to as the individual level of analysis or explanation. Questions posed at this level focus attention on biological, psychological, and socio-demographic characteristics of individuals, including—but not limited to—age, sex, race, education, employment, marital status, social attachments, commitment to the normative order and the law, intelligence, temperament, personality, and impulsivity (see Reiss and Roth 1993; Sampson and Lauritsen 1994). At the macrosocial level of explanation, scholars focus on what it is about various features of "organizations, social systems, social structures, and cultures that produces different rates" of violence (Short 1998:7). Scholars working at this level have asked such questioned as: Why do certain neighborhoods, cities, or states have elevated rates of violence relative to others?; Why do certain regions in the United States, such as the West and South, have elevated rates of violence relative to their Eastern and Northern counterparts?; and Why does the United States have elevated rates of violence relative to most other westernized nations? Finally, at the microsocial level, scholars ask about interaction processes and situational characteristics as they relate to the unfolding of criminal and violent incidents. Focus is on the immediate context in which behavior takes place. Most of this research addresses the role of such factors as the offender-victim relationship, affronts to one's honor and corresponding face-saving concerns and actions, behaviors of the victim, characteristics of the setting, third party presence and intervention, and the presence and use of alcohol, drugs, and weapons.

While all three levels of explanation have received some attention, theoretical and empirical emphases traditionally have been placed disproportionately on individual and macrosocial phenomena. Knowledge of microsocial phenomena is relatively limited.

THE MICROSOCIAL LEVEL IN CRIMINOLOGY
Despite a scholarly career focused primarily on individual criminals, Sutherland (1947:5) was among one of the first criminologists to recognize the potential import of microsocial factors when he distinguished between "historical" explanations of criminal behavior on one hand and "situational" explanations on the other. The former, he noted, focuses on "the processes operating in the earlier history of the criminal," whereas the latter implicates "processes which are operating at the moment of the occurrence of the crime" (Sutherland 1947:5). Sutherland chose not to pursue "situational" explanations, focusing instead on individual learning ("differential association") and cultural influences ("differential social organization"). Perhaps as a consequence, "historical" factors have held a virtual monopoly on the attention of criminologists.

For approximately two decades following Sutherland's distinction between historical and situational explanations of crime, little progress was made toward understanding the impact of microsocial factors on criminal and violent behaviors (Gibbons 1971). Aside from a few studies documenting the importance of the interaction between the "criminal and his victim" (von Hentig 1948; see also Bullock 1955; von Hentig 1940; Wolfgang 1957, 1958), interaction processes and situational characteristics continued to be overlooked both theoretically and empirically (Erez 1987). Birbeck and LaFree offer three reasons for the "neglected situation":

First, the sociological training of most criminologists leads them to think of the setting for crime in terms of broader social phenomena, for example, subcultures (Cohen 1955) and parenting styles (Hagan et al. 1985), rather than situations. Second, the obvious fact that individuals sometimes respond differently to the same situation (Thomas 1937) has encouraged criminologists to relegate situational experience to a status dependent on dispositions (Sutherland 1947:5). Finally, the systematic examination of situational variables is theoretically and methodologically complex, requiring the definition of key concepts, the development of conceptual models of the interaction between actors and situations, and the design of appropriate empirical research (Pervin 1981). (Birbeck and LaFree 1993:114)

By the mid- to late-1960s, disappointment over the poor predictive power of macrosocial and individual level explanations, and mounting evidence in experimental psychology (e.g., Berkowitz and LePage 1967; Brown 1968; see Carlson et al. 1990), led some scholars to question the implicit notion that microsocial factors are irrelevant or at least not very important in explaining crime and/or violence (Briar and Piliavin 1965; Cohen 1965; Wallace 1965; see Pittman and Handy 1964; Pokorny 1965). Hans Toch's (1969) landmark study, in which he emphasized the salience of interaction processes during violent encounters between police and civilians, provided further impetus to this trend.

Following Toch, a slight boom occurred in microsocial analyses, though much of this effort was contained outside of criminology (e.g., Banitt et al. 1970; Borden 1975; Borden and Taylor 1973; Borden et al. 1971; Buss et al. 1972; Curtis 1974; Gibbons 1971; Goode 1969; Halleck 1975; Hepburn 1973; Monahan 1975; Pecar 1972; Pervin 1976, 1978; Shoham 1972; Shoham et al. 1973; Silverman 1975; Taylor and Weinstein 1974; see also Ball-Rokeach 1973). Major developments within criminology occurred shortly thereafter, however, with the emergence of three theoretical perspectives—routine activities, rational choice, and social interactionism—that provided a complementary alternative to the historically-oriented theories dominating the field. All three of these theories "deal with transitory elements that come into play in immediate social contexts through which individuals pass" (Tittle and Paternoster 2000:434) and thus are rightly classified as situational theories. Routine activities and rational choice theories have been discussed at length elsewhere (see, e.g., Cohen and Felson 1979; Cornish and Clarke 1986) and will not be reviewed here. Of particular importance to this discussion is social interactionism. Social interactionism is similar to the other two theories in terms of its fundamental assumption that actors consider the costs and rewards of their actions before acting and its recognition of the importance of situational factors, such as third parties, characteristics of the victim, and the physical setting. It differs, however, in that attention is focused specifically on the *"patterns of interaction* between individuals and situations in the genesis of decisions to commit crime," particularly violent crime (Birbeck and LaFree 1993:130, emphasis added; see also Felson and Tedeschi 1993:1-2).

SOCIAL INTERACTIONISM

Although the roots of the social interactionist tradition in criminology can be traced back to the work of early labeling theorists (e.g., Tannenbaum 1938), current manifestations of this perspective were initiated by David Luckenbill's (1977) classic study of criminal homicide as a "situated transaction." In reviewing a variety of official documents surrounding 70 fatal transactions (including one double murder), which occurred in a medium-sized county in California between 1963 and 1972, Luckenbill (1977:176) discovered that, in all cases, "murder was the culmination of an interchange between an offender and victim, resembling what Goffman [1967] termed a 'character contest,' a confrontation in which opponents sought to establish or maintain 'face' at the other's expense by remaining steady in the face of adversity." Although others, such as Hepburn (1973) and Shoham and his colleagues (Shoham 1972; Shoham et al. 1973; see also Banitt et al. 1970) had previously drawn upon Goffman's notion of face-saving to explain violence in interpersonal relationships, Luckenbill's work received more scholarly recognition.

Following Luckenbill, a focus on interaction sequences and situational interpretations became more common, particularly as related to violent behavior. Within this interactionist framework, two approaches developed: symbolic interactionism and impression management theory.

SYMBOLIC INTERACTIONISM

Symbolic interactionism posits that (1) people respond to the symbolic environment on the basis of their "definitions of the situation"; (2) people behave on the basis of their perception of what the relevant audience evaluates positively (and not negatively); and (3) interactional outcomes are contingent on situational factors (Felson 1978:182-183).

Lonnie Athens' (1977, 1980) analyses of 58 male and female offenders convicted of at least one "substantially violent" criminal act are firmly rooted in this tradition. Both of his studies demonstrate how an actor's definition of the situation based on the interaction between one's self-image and taking the role of the victim as well as "the other" leads to distinct types of violent responses—physically defensive, frustrative, malefic, and frustrative-malefic. While intriguing, Athens' work did not have a significant impact on the discipline (see Rhodes 1999) and has been criticized on methodological and substantive grounds (see Birbeck and LaFree 1993:122-123).

Jack Katz's (1988) theory of "seductive crime" also exemplifies the symbolic interactionist approach by calling attention to the "foreground" factors contributing to deviant behavioral outcomes, all of which enable the perpetrators of such acts to "transcend" the reality of their limited life situations. In his discussion of "righteous slaughter," "sneaky thrills," the "badass," the "hardman," and the "cold-blooded killer," Katz emphasizes the unique appeal or "seductive qualities" of crimes associated with each category of "doing evil"; in the process, he demonstrates how deviant behavior can arise when self-identities are challenged in ongoing interaction.

IMPRESSION MANAGEMENT THEORY

Impression management theory shares the same basic assumptions as symbolic interactionism, but there is a crucial difference. Whereas the latter focuses on self-identities, the focus of the former is on social identities (Felson 1978, 1981). Unlike Athens and Katz, who stressed the importance of an internalized audience, impression management theory retains Goffman's (1955, 1967) and Luckenbill's (1977) emphasis on presentations of self made to an external audience and on corresponding observer attributions.

Development of the theory can be traced primarily through the work of Richard Felson and colleagues (Felson 1978, 1981, 1982, 1984, 1993; Felson and Steadman 1983; Felson and Tedeschi 1993; Felson et al. 1984, 1986), though other works identifying various stages of interpersonal disputes—naming (perception of injury), blaming (attribution of responsibility), and claiming (demand for remedy)— have made important contributions (Felstiner 1980-1981; Tedeschi and Nesler 1993; see also Luckenbill and Doyle 1989). Felson's work appears to have originated out of a desire to explain why it is that insults typically provoke aggressive retaliation, as had been demonstrated consistently in a number of empirical studies (see Felson 1978:206). Felson rejects the social learning notion that "[c]ounterattack or its threat reduces the probability that one will be attacked in the future, by demonstrating to others that such actions will be costly" (1978:207). He states:

> There are at least four reasons why such an explanation is inadequate for explaining many instances of retaliation. First, in many cases persons retaliate even when the material costs are high. Second, if preventing future attack is the only reason for counterattack it would be unnecessary to retaliate against persons we never expect to meet again. However, the evidence...clearly demonstrates that subjects retaliate against experimenters and confederates whom they know they are unlikely to see again. Third, since insulting others is generally an unacceptable and infrequent event, it is often unlikely that a counterinsult is necessary to prevent a further occurrence. Finally, evidence...suggests that subjects in competitive games counterattack even when they know their opponent's choices are preprogrammed and thus unalterable. (1978:207)

Felson (1978) suggests impression management theory as a more viable alternative. Aggression often is a means of saving face used by people when they are insulted—in many cases, inadvertently.[2] Social encounters, he argues, ordinarily are governed by an overarching

---

[2] There is a considerable amount of experimental evidence that aggressive retaliation is conditioned by whether or not intent is attributed to the initial transgressor (e.g., Epstein and Taylor 1967; Taylor and Pisano 1971).

"working consensus" among people, which obligates them to maintain politeness. However, situations sometimes arise in which individuals feel insulted by the real or perceived impoliteness of others (Felson 1978). In these cases, the offended party experiences "altercasting" (see Weinstein and Deutschberger 1963) or projection into an "unfavorable situational identity," which is characterized by a lack of "strength, competence, and courage" (Felson 1978:207). With the working consensus momentarily disrupted, the offended party feels free to abandon the rules of politeness and thereby initiate an aggressive counterattack against his/her antagonist(s). A successful counterattack allows the offended party to repair the damaged identity and recast it as deserving of higher regard or "honor" from the target and other observers. Felson (1978:209) mentions four situational alternatives to counterattack, however, the last three of which do not necessarily entail a loss of face: (1) accept the negative identity as legitimate and maybe apologize; (2) "back down" if costs are perceived as too high and maybe fantasize about retaliation; (3) "playing it cool" or "turning the other cheek" if that is what others appear to want; and (4) doing nothing, because the negative identity attribution has been nullified by (a) an apology from the antagonist, (b) the poor situational identity of the antagonist, and/or (c) third-party intervention as either mediator or protector (see also Banitt et al. 1970 for additional alternatives to counterattack, such as "selective perception" and "explaining away").

In 1981, Felson reiterated the basic thrust of his earlier work and drew more attention to the notion of aggression as social control, which Black (1983) would later develop more systematically. According to this argument, following the process of altercasting, the offended party will react aggressively in order to punish the transgressor for his/her illegitimate identity attack as well as to save face. If the punishment, in turn, is perceived as an identity attack, further retaliation is likely.

A series of empirical studies conducted by Felson and his colleagues (Felson 1982, 1984; Felson and Steadman 1983; Felson et al. 1984) provided considerable support for this interpretation. For example, in a study based on interviews with a representative sample from the general population (n = 245), a sample of ex-mental patients (n = 148), and a sample of ex-criminal offenders (n = 141), all drawn from a middle-sized New York state county, Felson (1982) found that, in general, respondents in all three samples reported that they were most likely to resort to aggressive behavior when they believed they had been insulted by their antagonist. This effect was particularly strong when both disputants were male and when third parties were present, a finding consistent with impression management theory if it is assumed that a heightened concern for situational identities exists among males due to the traditional emphasis placed on masculinity, toughness, bravery, etc. Additional analyses also revealed that certain face-saving devices, such as third-party mediation and "accounts" (see Scott and Lyman 1968) or other aligning actions (see Stokes and Hewitt 1976) offered by the antagonist, reduced the odds of retaliation, providing even further support.

Interaction processes and situational identities were also highlighted in a study of violent encounters described by 500 males incarcerated in New York State correctional facilities in 1977 and in 1978. Based on these data, Felson and Steadman (1983) describe violent encounters as a three-stage process in which "verbal conflict" and successful identity attacks lead to "threats and evasive action," which, in turn, lead to physical attack. As this study and a later study of a similar but smaller New York sample (N = 155) would also show, however, whether or not verbal conflicts escalate into violence often depends on the extent of encouragement provided by third parties (Felson and Steadman 1983; Felson et al. 1984).

Noting the limitations of the impression management approach to aggression and violence—i.e., its failure to explain aggression strategically undertaken to accrue a tangible reward or to avoid costs and its exclusive focus on retaliatory attacks—Felson (1984) suggested integrating impression management with his earlier notion of aggression as punishment and Tedeschi's notion of aggression as coercive power (see Brown and Tedeschi 1976; Tedeschi and Rosenfeld 1981; Tedeschi et al. 1974). Borrowing from each of the three approaches, Felson proposes the following scenario:

Aggressive encounters generally begin when persons violate norms or orders. The audience responds to these violations with an attack or threat to attack, either because they wish to produce compliance (by the target or third parties) or because they believe wrongdoing deserves to be punished. This initial attack can be described, then, as social control behavior. Once any attack of any kind occurs, identities and face-saving become involved and the likelihood of further attack is increased. However, the target of an attack may submit if he believes the costs of retaliation are too high. (1984:113)

Using data from his 1982 study, Felson (1984) found strong support for this integration. His analyses indicated that most aggressive encounters (about 90%) began with a norm or order violation, after which the offender punished the victim in order to maintain social control (the initial attack). Explicit identity attacks tended to occur later in the interaction sequence, "first as insults, then as threats, and then as physical attack" (Felson 1984:120).

In 1993, Felson distinguished between predatory violence and dispute-related violence and speculated on the different reasons for each (see also Felson and Tedeschi 1993). Unlike dispute-related violence, which Felson (1984) had previously shown to result from a desire to punish a norm violator, save face, or exercise coercive power as a form of deterrence, predatory violence is viewed as resulting from the perpetrator's desire to assert identity, coerce someone else to engage in or not engage in a certain behavior, and to restore equity. While these two types of violence clearly are different, Felson conceptualizes both as being goal-driven and, equally importantly, situationally induced.

Few studies address impression management theory and Felson's elaboration. As Tedeschi and Riordan (1981:243) state, "the main difficulty with the impression management theory is that it has been used to provide post hoc explanations for an available set of data and has not been seriously tested in transgression studies except for the Silverman et al. study." Twenty five years later, the situation is much the same.

In the Silverman et al. (1979) study, two experiments involving 93 female undergraduate subjects revealed that "prosocial" behavior following transgressions is more often used as a technique for impression management than as an attempt to relieve guilt or other negative affect. Although a number of later researchers recognized the importance of identity attacks in producing violent encounters among both males and females (e.g., Campbell 1982, 1986; Decker 1996; Fagan and Wilkinson 1998; Kleck and McElrath 1991; Kubrin and Weitzer 2003; Mullins et al. 2004; Savitz et al. 1991; Sommers and Baskin 1993), only a handful of empirical studies dealing specifically with impression management have been conducted. All of these studies are based on interview data, making them susceptible to problems stemming from social desirability effects, exaggeration, lying, recall, and so on.

First, results from Felson et al.'s (1986) study involving interviews with bartenders and bar owners in 67 Irish and 131 American bars showed that violent encounters were most likely to originate out of a dynamic exchange between bartenders acting as agents of control and intoxicated patrons, suggesting that "intoxication and the behaviors associated with it elicit from others a social-control reaction that is perceived as an affront by the intoxicated person, who then retaliates" (Felson et al. 1986:164). Intoxicated individuals may retaliate for any number of reasons other than to save face—e.g., disinhibition, frustration-aggression, etc. However, the "finding (in the American sample) that the age of a bar's clientele predicted the frequency of aggression in that bar, but that the participants in aggressive incidents were no younger than the general clientele" gives credence to an impression management interpretation, since, as Felson et al. (1986:164) argue, prior research "suggests that third parties in incidents of homicide and assault that involve youth are more likely to be supportive of violence and are likely to induce more intense violence."

In contrast, Berkowitz's (1978, 1986) studies based on interviews with men convicted of a violent assault and serving time, respectively, in an English or Scottish prison showed that saving face was at best a negligible factor in their professed reasons for committing the offense. Even though a number of respondents reported being aware of the audience during their violent incident, respondents most often attributed their aggression to safety concerns or a desire to hurt their antagonist.

Finally, similar findings were obtained by Oliver (1994), who interviewed an "opportunity sample" of 41 black male bar owners, bartenders, and bar patrons in an upstate New York city, all of whom had been involved in at least one violent confrontation or one potentially violent argument. The primary reason given for engaging in violence was not "to look good in front of the crowd" but to "avoid getting hurt" and to punish attackers for anti-normative behavior ("loud talking," getting bad," "insults and identity attacks," and "disrespect and unacceptable accounts") (Oliver 1994:102). Because he found numerous instances in which reference was made to the motivation provided by instigating third parties, however, Oliver questioned the accuracy of respondents' claims and emphasized instead the importance of the "reputational implications associated with unsuccessful management of interpersonal conflict in bars and bar settings" (1994:140).

SUMMARY

Increasing scholarly attention has been directed toward the microsocial level of explanation, and both theory and research suggest the importance of interaction sequences in which situated identities occupy a central position. Knowledge of the importance of situated identities under varied circumstances is still quite limited, however. More research is needed to clarify the interrelationships between interaction processes and other situational characteristics, not just in relation to the point of commission but also in relation to pre- and post-incident concerns, both of which have been shown to have important implications for criminal incidents (see Cusson 1993; Felson et al. 1999; Luckenbill 1977; Oliver 1994; Wilkinson 1998, 2003).

CHAPTER 2
Situational Correlates of Crime
A "Variable-Centered" Approach[3]

INTRODUCTION

Although theoretical developments at the microsocial level of explanation have been scarce, empirical attempts to identify situational correlates of crime have been more common. Progress in this area traditionally has been hindered by confusion over how to define the situational or microsocial level and the related difficulties of determining which features of specific events should be so classified (see Argyle et al. 1981; Sampson and Lauritsen 1994; Short 1998). However, general consensus has emerged that the focus of situational analyses should be on "*who* is involved, including the possibility that the individual is alone, *where* the action is taking place, and the nature of the *action* or activities occurring" (Pervin 1978:79-80, emphasis in original; see also Birbeck and LaFree 1993; LaFree and Birbeck 1991; Miethe and Meier 1994). The following variables have been identified as important situational correlates: setting, offender-victim relationship, victim behavior, third party presence and behavior, intoxicants, and weapons (see, e.g., Block 1981; Denno 1986; Miethe and Meier 1994; Monahan and Klassen 1982; Reiss and Roth 1993; Sampson and Lauritsen 1994). Co-offender and co-victim presence and behavior should be added to this list (see Hochstetler 2001; Warr 2002).

---

[3] According to Monahan and Klassen (1982:309, emphasis in original), a "variable-centered" perspective focuses on "what characteristics of situations in *general* relate to violent behavior." This is in contrast to a "situation-centered" perspective, which focuses on "how this particular situation influences different types of people to act."

17

SETTING

Prior research has demonstrated that some settings are more conducive to crime and violence than are others. Locations such as bars and taverns, cocktail lounges, and related establishments tend to have elevated rates of criminal activity (see Bullock 1955; Davidson 1989; Pokorny 1965; Steadman 1982; see also Roncek and Maier 1991). Prior research has also shown that a sizable proportion of serious violence occurs in other "loose," informal settings, such as in the streets and in many other public places (Bullock 1955; Davidson 1989; Luckenbill 1977; Miethe and Meier 1994; Pittman and Handy 1964; Steadman 1982).[4] A disproportionate convergence in these settings of the three key causal factors identified by routine activities theory—motivated offenders, attractive targets, and a lack of capable guardians—surely is part of the explanation. A more comprehensive explanation, however, must also take into account the impact that various settings have on interaction processes. Certain settings provide more opportunities for disputes to arise (see Short 1997:45), tend to attract more instigating— as opposed to mediating—third parties (see Felson et al. 1986), and are more permissive of "non-respectable" behaviors than are others (Luckenbill 1977:178), making identity attacks and aggressive retaliation more likely to occur. The setting of criminal and violent incidents is also important because it has been linked to a number of other situational correlates, such as the offender-victim relationship (Davidson 1989), choice and use of weapons (Wilkinson 1998, 2003), use of intoxicants (Fagan 1990a), level of victim-resistance (Block and Skogan 1986), and third party behavior (Felson et al. 1986).

---

[4] Block (1977) recommends caution in interpreting this finding due to the fact that non-stranger crimes (which are often committed indoors) and indoor crimes tend to be underreported in official data. However, studies based on other types of data have produced similar findings (Davidson 1989; Miethe and Meier 1994; Steadman 1982).

OFFENDER-VICTIM RELATIONSHIP

Despite conceptual and methodological problems (see Loftin et al. 1987; Williams and Flewelling 1988), research on the offender-victim relationship has produced several consistent findings. Research has shown that offender-victim relationships vary by offense type, with serious expressive acts such as homicide being more common among primary relations and instrumental acts such as robbery more common among non-primary relations (Cook 1987; Williams and Flewelling 1988; cf. Decker 1996). Research has also demonstrated the intra-racial nature of most violent crimes and the tendency of both male and female offenders to have male victims (see Sampson and Lauritsen 1994). None of this research, however, has examined how the offender-victim relationship operates at the microsocial level. As Goode (1969:953) notes, "[t]his direction of inquiry has been neglected in the past, because official records contain few usable data on the actual processes through which violence was generated; because of our propensity to find a guilty party; and of course because the social researcher cannot easily locate a sample of violent acts for field observation." Although Goode (1969: 953) was referring specifically to violence among intimates, his criticism is apposite for all types of violent encounters. More attention needs to be directed toward the impact of the offender-victim relationship on interaction sequences. Interpretations of different behaviors clearly are conditioned by the nature of the social relationship between relevant actors (Mummendey and Otten 1993), with identity attacks committed in front of others by a person of equal status appearing to be especially likely to lead to aggressive retaliation (Luckenbill and Doyle 1989; see also Gould 2003). Evidence also suggests that conditional relationships exist between the offender-victim relationship and other situational correlates, such as setting (Davidson 1989; Miethe and Meier 1994; Silverman and Kennedy 1987), intoxicants (Pernanen 1991), and the choice and use of certain types of weaponry (Silverman and Kennedy 1987).

VICTIM BEHAVIOR

Within criminology, it is often assumed that the victim of crime or violence frequently plays a critical role in the genesis and severity of his/her own victimization (see Mendelsohn 1963; von Hentig 1940, 1948; see also Gottfredson 1989; Schafer 1968; Sparks 1982 for more detailed reviews). Empirical analyses tend to support this assumption.

Individuals commonly contribute to the occurrence of a criminal or violent incident in which they end up as "the victim" (Amir 1971; Curtis 1974; Felson and Steadman 1983; Luckenbill 1977; Savitz et al. 1991; Wallace 1965; Wolfgang 1957, 1958). This generally happens in two ways. First, by initiating a transaction—whether intended or not—through a verbal or physical norm-violation,[5] which the target (i.e., the person eventually classified as "the offender") then perceives as an identity attack or as a behavior that needs to be met with a punishment or a display of coercive power (Felson 1984), victims of violent encounters can directly trigger the violence that leads to their own injury or demise. Second, by engaging in any number of routine activities, victims either knowingly or unknowingly make themselves available, suitable, and/or vulnerable targets (see Sparks 1982).

Victim behaviors also influence the degree to which violent incidents escalate. The extent (none versus some) and type (forceful versus non-forceful) of resistance offered by a victim, particularly during robberies and rapes, have been related to the severity of injuries sustained in and the successful completion of an attack (Block 1977, 1981; Block and Skogan 1986; Felson and Steadman 1983; Luckenbill 1980). Felson (1978) and others (Oliver 1994; Tedeschi and Riordan 1981) have also shown that the victim can reduce the likelihood of violence by offering accounts or engaging in other aligning actions, which mitigate the effect of the initial identity attack[6] and decrease the likelihood that intervening third parties will be personally offended by non-compliance to their request for an "acceptable account."

---

[5] Some authors consider victim-precipitation to have occurred only if the victim was the first to engage in a physical attack against the eventual offender (e.g., Wolfgang 1957, 1958), while others have broadened the definition to include verbal attacks as well as insinuating gestures (e.g., Curtis 1974; Sparks 1982).

[6] Felson (1984) found that, when they are offered, accounts tend to follow, not precede, a reproach. Thus, excuses or justifications for the commission of behavior that another individual finds offensive typically do not occur until the offended party has censured the guilty actor.

Clearly, victim behavior is often a key factor in violent incidents. "Many victims might have avoided being the subject of violence if they had altered their behavior in some critical way" (Halleck 1975:37). This is at least partly because such behavioral alterations are likely to have important implications for situated identities as well as for the operation of at least some of the other situational correlates, such as the setting, offender-victim relationship, and the presence of intoxicants and co-offenders and co-victims (Block and Skogan 1986; Wolfgang 1957; but see Felson and Messner 1998; Felson and Steadman 1983).

THIRD PARTIES

A number of studies have examined the role of third parties (presence or behavior) in interpersonal encounters. Much of this work has occurred within the domain of experimental psychology, where research findings have been supportive of impression management theory in two important ways. First, research has consistently shown that subjects tend to act in accordance with the expressed values of third parties, with aggressive retaliation more likely in front of third parties favoring such behavior and less likely when third parties favor a more pacifist response (Borden and Taylor 1973; see Brown 1968; Rubin 1980). When the values of third parties are not expressed and therefore are unknown, subjects tend to act in accordance with values they impute to the third parties on the basis of such social characteristics as sex and social status (Borden 1975; Richardson et al. 1979; see Borden and Taylor 1973). Second, experimental research suggests that intervening third parties "facilitate concession making without loss of face, thereby promoting more rapid and effective conflict resolution than would otherwise occur" (Rubin 1980:380; see also Pruitt and Johnson 1970). Ostensibly, this is because third-party intervention provides subjects with a legitimate reason for backing down from a threatening situation, a behavior that might be attributed to a lack of bravery or honor if done under other circumstances (see Cooney 1998).

While these two findings are consistent with impression management theory in the sense that they both show—albeit in different ways—that behavior often is motivated by a desire to look good, or at least not look bad, in front of other people, Felson et al. note that the generalizability or external validity of these studies may be limited:

> First, it is difficult if not impossible to get subjects to engage in aggressive behavior in experiments without making it appropriate through some instructional set...Second, it has been demonstrated that subjects are extremely vulnerable to social influence in experimental situations...Third, experiments may use extreme stimulus values in their manipulations that rarely if ever occur in natural setting. (1984:453)

Non-experimental research has also produced evidence supportive of impression management theory. Most of this research is based on official data and, perhaps for this reason, focuses almost exclusively on completed violent crimes, particularly homicides and/or assaults (see below for a critical discussion of this approach). Nevertheless, the consistency of findings produced by these studies warrants at least some confidence.

At a descriptive level, research based on diverse samples has shown that third parties are present in a substantial proportion of violent incidents that eventually come to the attention of researchers (Felson and Steadman 1983; Luckenbill 1977; Oliver 1994; Sommers and Baskin 1993), a finding hardly surprising when one considers that (1) these incidents tend to occur in public settings and (2) third parties often actively encourage the conflict (Felson et al. 1984), perhaps in many cases because of their relationship with the offender, victim, or both (Decker 1995; Oliver 1994).

Third parties do not always act in ways that instigate, facilitate, escalate, or otherwise promote a violent outcome amongst two disputants, even though there is evidence to suggest that this is common (Felson and Steadman 1983; Luckenbill 1977; Sommers and Baskin 1993; see also Cooney 1998). Other roles taken by third parties may also affect the way interaction sequences unfold.

First, third parties may become so involved with the conflict that they end up as "the victim" or "the offender" (co-offenders and co-victims will be discussed later). Decker (1995) refers to this as the "witnesses as surrogates" category. People who have an intimate relationship with at least one of the participants are the most likely to fall into this category.

Second, third parties may attempt to mediate, though this may be less common than the encourager role (Felson and Steadman 1983; Sommers and Baskin 1993; cf. Wallace 1965). It is assumed that third party mediation reduces the odds (or severity) of a violent outcome because this type of intervention not only represents explicit disapproval of violence but also provides disputants with the opportunity to back down without losing face (Felson 1978; Hepburn 1973). Research rarely examines the effect of third parties on variations in outcomes (e.g., violent versus non-violent), making it impossible to estimate the general success of third party mediation. However, some research has focused on slight differences in severity. Results show that third party mediation generally reduces subsequent aggression (Felson 1982), including the number of blows thrown by offenders in events leading either to assault or murder (Felson et al. 1984). At the same time, third party mediation has been shown to have no effect on whether the victim is killed or only assaulted (Felson and Steadman 1983). Perhaps further insight will emerge from research focusing on the point of mediation in an interaction sequence (see Felson and Steadman 1983; Luckenbill 1977:184), the relationship of third parties to both the offender and the victim (see Felson 1993; Felson et al. 1984), the target(s) of mediation (Oliver 1994:99), and a wider range of possible outcomes.

Finally, third parties may remain totally neutral, neither encouraging, mediating, nor otherwise involving themselves in the conflict. Research on the impact of "bystanders" on the situational dynamics of violent encounters is rare, perhaps because third parties tend to take more active roles (Decker 1995). In one study, Decker (1995) found that bystanders constitute the smallest category of all possible witness roles and that most of them are strangers to both the offender and the victim. Earlier, Steadman (1982) found that the more third parties are present, the more conflicts tend to escalate from verbal to hitting disputes and from hitting to weapons disputes. Without more information, this finding is subject to several interpretations. It could be that the mere presence of an audience does in fact increase the severity of violence, because the need to maintain face is enhanced when people other than antagonist are observing the incident. Alternatively, as Steadman (1982) seems to suggest, it could be that increases in severity lead to increases in the number of third parties present rather than vice versa. It could also be that the lack of a control for third party behavior in Steadman's study resulted in an artifactual finding. Finally, the characteristics of the third parties may have served as cues prompting further violence. Had other types of third parties been present, events might have unfolded differently.

Despite such confusion, ample evidence—experimental as well as non-experimental—has demonstrated the importance of third parties in interpersonal encounters. Since research has shown that third parties tend to be present in a substantial proportion of violent encounters (which eventually come to the attention of researchers), it is imperative that more theoretical and empirical attention be given to the different roles that third parties choose to take and the impact of these decisions on incident outcome.

INTOXICANTS

Alcohol and other drugs have been linked to aggressive and even violent behaviors as well as to victimization in both experimental and non-experimental research (see Blum 1981; Collins 1983; Fagan 1990a for reviews). Within criminology, a long line of research has shown that intoxicants: (1) are associated with an increased risk of victimization and more severe injuries to victims (e.g., Felson and Steadman 1983; Wolfgang 1958; see Collins 1983) and (2) are present—among offenders, victims, or both—in a substantial proportion of both officially recorded and undetected violent offenses (see Collins 1983; Fagan 1990a). Thus, that a relationship exists between intoxicants and aggressive/violent behavior is generally beyond dispute, though some have pointed to methodological problems (e.g., Gibbs 1986; Greenberg 1981; Pernanen 1991) or the possibility of "spuriousness" or "common cause" explanations as reasons to proceed with caution (Pernanen 1981; see also Collins 1981).

Despite the overwhelming cross-discipline consensus concerning the alcohol-aggressive/violent behavior association, scholars have yet to agree on how best to account for this empirical regularity, as indicated by the sheer number of possible explanations suggested in the literature (on alcohol and drugs, see Fagan 1990a; on alcohol only, see Pernanen 1981; on drugs only, see Goldstein 1989). Fagan (1990a) has classified these explanations into four categories: (1) biological, which implicates neural, endocrinological, or other physiological responses to intoxication as the direct cause of aggressive or violent behavior; (2) psychopharmacological, which points to the interaction between intoxicants and the individual psyche as conducive to aggressive or violent behavior; (3) psychological and psychiatric, which suggests that personality or psychopathological alterations produced by intoxicants can lead to aggressive or violent behavior; and (4) social and cultural, which do not deny the validity of the other types of explanations but which emphasize the need to consider the role of social factors as well. These perspectives will not be reviewed here, since they have received extensive treatment elsewhere (see Fagan 1990a). Suffice it to say that each has found some support but that no single type of explanation by itself has been shown to be completely adequate. As Fagan (1990a:287) notes, "there is little empirical evidence within or across disciplines to support the separate explanations of the precise causal mechanisms by which the measurable effects of intoxication may lead to specific aggressive behaviors."

Limited attention to the impact of intoxicants on the situational dynamics of interpersonal encounters may help explain this lack of clarity (Roman 1981; Watters et al. 1985). This is especially true in criminology, where knowledge of the effect of intoxicants on criminal and violent incidents has not advanced much beyond the conclusions of earlier work, which suggested that cultural rituals or precepts can and often do affect "drunken comportment" in drinking situations (Levinson 1983a; MacAndrew and Edgerton 1969; but see Parker 1993, 1995). While a few scholars have acknowledged the importance of such microsocial variables as the permissiveness of the drinking setting as well as the number of people present and the relationships among them (e.g., Levinson 1983b), only rarely do they provide more than a simplistic explanation of their effects. In his attempt at an integrative model of substance use and aggression, for example, Fagan (1990a) states that cultural factors influence the setting and social context of drinking situations, which in turn influence both the rules and norms of behavior and cognitive interpretations of the situation, thereby affecting the probability of aggression. This multi-level conceptualization is a good start, but it is too imprecise to be entirely satisfying. More information is needed on the specific behavioral effects of microsocial factors and the circumstances under which they are most likely occur. Hepburn (1973:425; see also Gibbs 1986; Fagan 1993) suggested earlier that the ingestion of intoxicants, especially alcohol, often leads to violence because of the increase in (perceived or actual) identity attacks associated with the "breakdown in taken-for-granted patterns of accountability and claiming behavior" and a concomitant decrease in the ability to deal with such attacks in a non-violent manner. Unfortunately, this interpretation of the intoxication-violence relationship has not yet been subjected to direct empirical testing. Research by Oliver (1994) and Fagan and Wilkinson (1998), however, indicate that participants in violent encounters readily attribute their behavior to the role played by intoxicants in heightening their sensitivity to rule-violations by others and diminishing their ability to respond less severely to minor provocations. In Oliver's (1994) study, several respondents also blamed alcohol intoxication for the rule-violations committed by their antagonists (see also Felson and Steadman 1983). Together, what these findings suggest is that the empirically established relationship between intoxicants and aggressive/violent behavior may be at least partially explained by the impact of intoxicants at various stages of interaction.

Overall, then, a considerable amount of research has demonstrated a link between intoxicants and aggressive or violent behavior, and numerous explanations of this relationship have been advanced. However, none of these explanations have performed adequately when applied to drinking situations occurring in varying social contexts. At least part of the problem is the almost universal neglect of the role of intoxicants at the microsocial level. What little research that has been done clearly suggests that intoxicants affect the behavior of participants in ongoing interaction, and future research will probably reveal that this effect conditions and/or is conditioned by the impact of all or at least some of the other situational variables.

WEAPONS

Knowledge about the role of weapons in criminal incidents comes largely from research on robbery, homicide, and, to a lesser extent, rape (Block and Skogan 1986; Cook 1979, 1981, 1987; Kleck and McElrath 1991; Skogan 1978; but see Wells and Horney 2002). Although there are slight differences by offense type, much of this research has shown that the presence of weaponry (in most cases, firearms) is negatively related to risk of injury but positively related to severity of injury. Not denying the importance of offender motivation, scholars typically have explained this finding by pointing to the situational characteristics of incidents involving weapons. Depending on the nature of the crime, two major variants appear in the literature.

For "predatory" violence, such as robbery and rape, the suggested interaction sequence occurs as follows (see Block and Skogan 1986; Luckenbill 1980; see also Baumer et al. 2003). An offender initiates the incident by brandishing a weapon, which is done primarily to gain control or mastery over the situation. Since the threat of lethal violence is more credible when the offender is armed, the victim is less likely to resist, enabling the offender to complete the offense without further use of force and thus explaining why injury is less likely when weapons are present. If the victim chooses to resist, however, the offender is forced to back up his/her threat with violence in order to accomplish the goal of completing the attack. Obviously, the consequences usually will be more serious when a weapon is involved than when a weapon is not involved, thus explaining why severe injuries are more likely when weapons actually are employed.

For "dispute-related" violence, the following sequence has been suggested (Fagan and Wilkinson 1998; Kleck and McElrath 1991; see also Baumer at al. 2003). The eventual victim intentionally or unintentionally insults the eventual offender. Whether instantaneously or after additional verbal exchanges, the offender brandishes the weapon to demonstrate to the victim and to any observers that he/she is a powerful individual who deserves respect. Since the offender is armed, the victim is unlikely to resist, especially because the presence of a weapon provides a socially acceptable reason for withdrawing from the conflict. As stated by Kleck and McElrath (1991:674), "[t]he failure to retaliate, which might otherwise be regarded by witnesses as evidence of cowardice, is viewed instead as mere prudence in the face of greatly unequal power." Thus, temporarily relieved from status concerns, the victim is much less likely to challenge the offender and is therefore much less likely to be injured. However, if the victim still chooses to resist—perhaps because he/she, too, is armed and feels compelled to counteract the process of altercasting—the offender is likely to interpret this behavior as an identity attack and will attempt to save face by using the weapon and thus seriously injuring the victim.

Although the explanations offered to explain predatory and dispute-related incidents involving weapons differ in terms of their point of emphasis, with practical features playing a greater part in the former and symbolic features playing a greater part in the latter, both alert us to the possibility that dynamic processes occurring in the immediate context have important implications for the outcome of potentially violent incidents. Both explanations suggest that the behavior of one participant in a social interaction may impact the behavior of the other, and vice versa. Thus, by altering the behavior of either or both of the participants, independently or perhaps through conditional relationships with some of the other microsocial variables, weapons are likely to affect the manner in which the interaction unfolds.

CO-OFFENDERS AND CO-VICTIMS

Research clearly suggests that the presence of co-offenders and co-victims can alter the dynamics of a criminal incident (Clark 1995; Farrington 1998; Farrington et al. 1982; Felson and Messner 1996), yet co-offenders and co-victims are almost never included in general discussions of microsocial variables (e.g., see Sampson and Lauritsen 1994). This may be due to the fact that it is sometimes difficult to distinguish co-offenders and co-victims from third parties, especially those third parties who participate actively. Unlike third parties, however, co-offenders and co-victims do not simply encourage or mediate between the offender and victim; they also act or are treated as key participants in the incident. As a result, they are likely to affect the development and maintenance of situated identities and influence other situational characteristics, such as victim behavior and use of weapons (see Farrington 1998; Farrington et al. 1982). In order to understand how a particular interaction sequence unfolds, then, it is important to consider the presence and behavior of co-offenders and co-victims.

CHAPTER 3

The Microsocial Level in Gang Research

INTRODUCTION

As in the general criminological literature, research on youth street gangs has focused primarily on the macrosocial and individual levels of explanation (see Hughes forthcoming). This has led to a number of important insights about the "types of places" (typically disorganized) in which gangs thrive and the "kinds of people" (often socially disabled and disadvantaged) who populate these groupings. In contrast to general criminology, however, the gang literature also has a fairly strong microsocial emphasis. At least part of the reason for this stems from the fact that gang studies are firmly rooted in the Chicago school tradition and are therefore characterized by sensitivity to "process" and observations made "*in situ*" (Short 1998). By attending to behaviors as they unfold in their natural setting, gang researchers have been able to document some of the more dynamic properties of gang delinquency, most of which are missed in studies based on other types of research methods. These dynamic properties are commonly referred to as "group processes," and two in particular have been proposed as being crucial to our understanding of the way criminal, especially violent, incidents unfold among delinquent street gangs: status management and group cohesiveness.

STATUS MANAGEMENT

The notion of status management—that is, achieving status or protecting status that has already been achieved—can be seen as impression management theory tailored specifically to youth culture, particularly as manifested in the streets. Consistent with impression management theory, the focus is on the motivation produced by the desire to look good and avoid looking bad in front of others, only here the emphasis is on an audience made up primarily of one's peers.

Status vis-à-vis one's peers has long been recognized as a major source of conflict among youth. As early as 1927, Thrasher directed attention to the constant struggle for status among gang members:

> Internally the gang may be viewed as a struggle for recognition. It offers the underprivileged boy probably his best opportunity to acquire status and hence it plays an essential part in the development of his personality...[T]he gang boy's conception of his role is more vivid with reference to his gang than to other social groups. Since he lives largely in the present he conceives of the part he is playing in life as being in the gang; his status in other groups is unimportant to him, for the gang is his social world. In striving to realize the role he hopes to take he may assume a tough pose, commit feats of daring or of vandalism, or become a criminal. (1963: 230-231)

Although status management remained prominent in later gang literature (see, for example, Whyte 1943), theories advanced by Cohen (1955), Miller (1958) and Cloward and Ohlin (1960) directed attention away from status in relation to the gang world toward a larger class system context. Research designed explicitly to test these theories, however, found that status considerations within the gang context were more immediately significant to understanding the behavior of gang members (Short and Strodtbeck, 1965). Observations of gang conflicts suggested that violent behavior was frequently initiated in response to status threats, that is, threats to the respect or honor one deserves "as a leader, as a male, as a member of a particular gang, or as an aspiring adult" (Short 1965:162). Decisions by gang members, especially leaders, to fight were attributed in part to the rational balancing of immediate status losses or gains within the gang against the more remote possibility of punishment by the larger society.

Later work on male and female gangs representing a variety of ethnic backgrounds reaffirmed Short and Strodtbeck's (1965) earlier conclusions regarding status in relation to one's peers as a major factor in the genesis of violence (e.g., Anderson 1990, 1998; Campbell 1991; Cartwright et al. 1971; Erlanger 1979; Giordano 1978; Horowitz and Schwartz 1974; Vigil 1988; see also Cartwright et al. 1975), even when not recognized explicitly (e.g., Jankowski 1991). Elijah Anderson's (1999) urban ethnography, *Code of the Streets*, further alerted gang researchers to the salience of the subcultural value system or "street code" that develops in the inner-city and emphasizes violence as a means to achieve or maintain respect (or status). As gang research has moved away from the "contextualist" tradition of the Chicago school, however, analyses of the status management process and its behavioral influence have been noticeably lacking (see Hughes forthcoming). Moreover, interrelations between status and other microsocial variables are rarely explored. While status considerations have been linked to fights over "turf" and have also been shown to affect and be affected by the presence and use of intoxicants and weapons (Fagan and Wilkinson 1998; Vigil 1988; Wilkinson 1998, 2003), only recently have researchers begun to investigate the possibility that the relationship between status considerations and these types of delinquent behaviors is contingent on other microsocial variables (see Hughes and Short 2005). This may explain why, despite the fact that numerous studies support the existence of a facilitative gang effect (see Battin et al. 1998; Esbensen and Huizinga 1993; Thornberry et al. 1993, 2003), explanation of the processes within the gang that promote such facilitation are noticeably absent.

COHESIVENESS

Although group cohesiveness has been defined and measured in different ways, scholars generally use the term to refer to the degree to which members are attracted to the group as a whole and to other group members. According to Lucore (1975:92), "the more cohesive the group, the greater will be its members' desire to remain members and contribute to and participate in it, thus strengthening the group." Cohesiveness can be thought of as a relatively stable group characteristic (Cartwright et al. 1975:5), but it has also been recognized as "the quintessential group process" (Klein 1995:43), with important implications for understanding delinquent activities.

Although research has consistently found a relationship between group cohesiveness and gang delinquency (but see Morash 1983), the nature of the relationship remains unclear. Cohesiveness and gang delinquency have been found to be both positively (Klein 1971, 1995; Klein and Crawford 1967) and negatively related (Cartwright et al. 1970; Jankowski 1991; Jansyn 1966). Short (1997:117-118) argues that this contradiction is "more apparent than real," and he suggests reconciling these discrepant findings by taking into account differences among the gangs studied, particularly their "history of cohesiveness" and the extent to which they were influenced by the behavior of a detached gang worker. Not denying the possibility of a reciprocal relationship (Lucore 1975:96), I argue further that the operation of other microsocial variables (i.e., not just third parties) may also be relevant.

With the exception of third parties and intoxicants, research has yet to explore the relationship between group cohesiveness and other microsocial variables. Klein's study (1971; see also Klein 1995) of a variety of gangs in Los Angeles demonstrated how third parties—in this case, detached workers—can affect group cohesiveness, and Vigil's (1988:126) study of Chicano gangs in Southern California showed how the consumption of alcohol or drugs act as a "social lubricant to facilitate the broadening, deepening, and solidifying of group affiliations and cohesiveness." Since intoxicants and third parties have been linked in other studies to status considerations (Fagan and Wilkinson 1998; Rubin 1980; Vigil 1988), it is reasonable to suggest that cohesiveness and status considerations are related (see Lucore 1975:98). However, neither the nature of this relationship nor how it is related to delinquency has been established, and the possibility that the relationship between cohesiveness and delinquency is contingent on other microsocial variables has not been examined.

SUMMARY

The influence of the Chicago school is perhaps most evident in the gang literature, where the microsocial level of explanation has received a considerable amount of attention. Group processes (i.e., status management and cohesiveness) are suggested to be crucial to understanding delinquency as it occurs in the gang milieu. However, the etiological significance of group processes is unlikely to be fully realized until more is known about the complex relationships that exist among these and other microsocial phenomena, and how such relationships affect delinquency. Only then will we be able to see how macrosocial factors (e.g., social disorganization, lack of legitimate opportunities, etc.) in combination with individual level factors (e.g., social disabilities, etc.) are translated at the microsocial level into specific behaviors at particular times and places (see Hughes forthcoming).

CHAPTER 4

Research Issues

INTRODUCTION

While scholarly interest in microsocial analyses has increased in recent years, progress has been hindered by the failure to investigate *both* violent and non-violent outcomes as well as by a disconnect between empirical analyses and a unifying framework from which results may be interpreted. The current research is both a theory testing and a theory building effort. Whereas the former is oriented toward assessment of the extent to which hypotheses derived from impression management theory are supported, the latter is oriented toward further development of impression management theory as a conceptual scheme from which to understand and explain the effect of microsocial factors on the occurrence of disputes and on their (violent and non-violent) outcomes. The specific hypotheses to be tested are listed below. Results for each are presented in Chapter 6, along with findings from exploratory analysis of interaction sequences.

Hypothesis 1: There will be a positive association between territory and dispute outcome. That is, dispute-related incidents that occur in the turf of one party but not the other will be more likely to escalate into violence than will be dispute-related incidents that occur in more neutral settings.

Routine activities theory and research suggest that opportunities for violent encounters are most likely to occur in settings in which there is a convergence of potential offenders, suitable victims, and a lack of capable guardians. Coupled with the fact that the data consist mainly of detached worker and observer reports of activities witnessed while spending time with gang members in the field, this leads to the expectation that dispute-related incidents will occur most often in "loose" settings in which offenders and victims regularly interact with one another and/or others. In the gang context, these places are public and generally located near the homes of both the offender and victim (e.g., street corners and poolrooms).

From an impression management perspective, however, violence can be seen as a means of extending or defending individual or group status, both of which are likely to be involved in disputes that occur in one—and only one—party's turf (the party with the territorial claim acting in defense of status and the opposing party acting so as to enhance status). Thus, these types of disputes are expected to be the most likely to escalate into violence. The likelihood of non-violent outcomes should be higher for disputes that occur in settings in which neither party has a more legitimate claim to ownership, as status concerns will not be as intense because rights to territory are unlikely to be at stake.

Hypothesis 2: There will be a positive association between offender-victim gang relationship and dispute outcome. That is, dispute-related incidents involving members of rival gangs will be more likely to escalate into violence than will be dispute-related incidents involving all other types of offender-victim gang relationships.

Previous gang research suggests that aggression is most often an intra-group phenomenon (Miller et al. 1961). In part, this is a function of the amount of time spent among group members. Since members of adolescent street gangs tend to spend more of their time together than with other people, there are more opportunities for disputes to occur in this context than in any other. According to impression management theory, however, frequency of dispute occurrence does not determine dispute outcome. Rather, the likelihood that disputes will result in violence should be greatest when status considerations are most pressing and should decrease as status considerations become less relevant. Because disputes between members of rival gangs are the only context in which individual and gang status are both at stake, these types of disputes are expected to be the most likely to have violent outcomes. The outcome of intra-gang disputes may be contingent on the similarities or differences in the rank of the participating gang members (i.e., core on core, core on fringe, fringe on core, or fringe on fringe), but intra-gang disputes generally should be less likely than rival gang disputes to escalate into violence, because individual status concerns are not compounded by considerations of gang status in disputes between members of the same gang. Excessive violence among members of a single gang can also threaten group cohesiveness and therefore result in a loss of status among either or both disputants (see Miller et al. 1961). In addition, mediation by detached workers and other third parties probably is more likely in intra-gang disputes than in disputes between members of rival gangs due to the nature of the relationship and also proximity during interaction. Overall, then, the probability that rival gang disputes will result in violence is expected to be higher than is the case for disputes involving all other types of offender-victim gang relationships, even those that are likely to occur more frequently.

Hypothesis 3a: The greatest proportion of dispute-related incidents will begin with a norm- or order-violation on the part on the victim.

Hypothesis 3b: There will be a positive association between victim resistance (including threats, explicit identity attacks, non-compliance, etc.) and dispute outcome.

Hypothesis 3c: There will be a negative association between the provision of accounts or other aligning actions on the part of the victim and dispute outcome.

According to the social interactionist perspective, conflicts between people often emerge in the form of a "character contest," the initial stage of which involves the victim saying something and/or behaving in such a way that the offender feels is insulting or otherwise needs to be met with punishment. Thus, in these data, non-compliant and other inappropriate behaviors on the part of the victim are expected to constitute the most common reason for the occurrence of dispute-related incidents. Whether such incidents escalate into violence or are resolved non-violently, however, should depend on the manner in which the victim responds to the offender's attempt to maintain face and/or social control (the initial attack). Because victim resistance following the initial attack increases the stakes of the character contest by directly calling the offender's situated identity into question, it is expected to increase the likelihood that disputes will escalate into violence.[7] On the other hand, if the victim offers an account or otherwise behaves in a way that mitigates the process of altercasting, status considerations should become less pressing, thereby resulting in a higher likelihood of a non-violent outcome.

Hypothesis 4a: The greatest proportion of dispute-related incidents will occur in the presence of a third party.

Hypothesis 4b: There will be a positive association between third party behavior and dispute outcome. That is, third party instigation will be related to violent outcomes, whereas third party mediation/protection will be associated with non-violent outcomes.

Hypothesis 4c: Dispute-related incidents that occur in the presence of male youth bystanders will be more likely to escalate into violence than will be dispute-related incidents that occur in the presence of other types of bystanders.

Since the presentation of an acceptable self made to an external audience is considered by impression management theory to be a crucial factor in the emergence of character contests, the data should reveal a strong tendency for dispute-related incidents to develop in the presence of third parties. Although supportive findings may be at least partly accounted for by the fact that dispute-related incidents that come to the attention of observers are more likely than unobserved disputes to occur in (public) settings where third parties are apt to be present, impression management theory suggests that such findings also reflect the desire among disputants to maintain face in front of other people.

---

[7] Although "the victim" may attack "the offender" immediately after being punished, Felson's (1984) research suggests that this occurs infrequently. Nevertheless, the current research takes this possibility into account.

In addition, impression management theory claims that the role taken by members of the external audience will have a strong influence on the unfolding of disputes. This is because disputants are likely to feel that, in order to maintain an acceptable situated identity, they must act in accordance with the expectations of key observers. Thus, when third parties engage in instigating behavior, status concerns become more pressing for disputants—the offender, victim, or both, depending on the target of the third party instigation—and the likelihood of a violent dispute outcome should thereby increase. When third parties attempt to mediate/protect, however, they not only make explicit their disapproval of violence but also provide the target(s) of their efforts with a reason for backing down from violence other than a lack of honor. Consequently, a non-violent outcome is more likely. The influence of bystanders is expected to vary according to their socio-demographic characteristics, because disputants are apt to impute certain values to these non-active third parties and behave accordingly. Research indicates that pro-violence values are more often attributed to males and youths than to females and older persons (Borden 1975; see also Felson et al. 1984), and "status management" in front of one's gang peers—who typically are male youth—has been suggested as one of the most salient factors in the development of violence (Short and Strodtbeck 1965). Hence, disputes that emerge in the presence of male youth bystanders are predicted to be more likely than disputes that emerge in the presence of all other types of bystanders to escalate into violence.

Hypothesis 5: There will be a positive association between the number of parties in dispute-related incidents under the influence of intoxicants and dispute outcome.

One implication of impression management theory is that the ingestion of intoxicants is likely to be associated with violence because of its tendency to bring about a breakdown in taken-for-granted interaction patterns. Such a breakdown makes the commission and perception of identity attacks more likely and, at the same time, decreases the likelihood that these transgressions can and will be effectively dealt with in a non-violent manner. Therefore, as the number of parties to a dispute who have ingested intoxicants increases, the likelihood of violence should also increase.

Hypothesis 6: The possession and threatened use of weaponry by both parties of a dispute will be associated with violent outcomes, whereas the possession and threatened use of weaponry by only one party will be associated with non-violent outcomes.

If impression management theory is accurate, the data should reveal a twofold effect of weapons in interpersonal disputes. On one hand, when only one party of a dispute is armed, the likelihood of a violent outcome will be reduced, since the unfair advantage possessed by the armed party provides the unarmed party with an opportunity to back down from violence (that clearly carries with it a high level of cost) without suffering a consequential loss of face. Under these circumstances, withdrawal is considered to be more prudent decision than engagement and not one that reflects a lack of honor. As quoted by Kleck and McElrath (1991:674), "Only a fool attacks a man with a gun." On the other hand, however, when both parties introduce weapons into the dispute, the stakes of the "character contest" will have increased to the point at which withdrawal by either party certainly would result in a loss of face, thus making violence more likely to result.

Hypothesis 7a: There will be a positive association between co-offender presence and dispute outcome.

Hypothesis 7b: There will be a positive association between co-offender instigation and dispute outcome.

Hypothesis 7c: There will be a positive association between co-victim instigation and dispute outcome.

Similar to instigating third parties, co-offender presence should increase the likelihood of violent behavior, particularly if these co-offenders engage in instigating behavior. In order to maintain an acceptable situated identity, the offender must act in accordance with either implicit or explicit expectations of violence, which will be conveyed, respectively, by the mere presence of co-offenders and their more active ways of offering encouragement or other forms of support.

In contrast, the likelihood of non-violent outcomes will be higher when an offender is acting alone, since the pressure to maintain one's honor through the use of force will not be as great. Precise predictions about the impact of co-victim presence on dispute outcome cannot be made at this time due to the lack of theoretical as well as empirical guidance. However, if co-victims encourage or otherwise support the use of violence, the victim is apt to feel compelled to behave accordingly in order to avoid losing face, thereby increasing the likelihood of a violent dispute outcome.

CHAPTER 5

Data and Methods

DATA

Over a three-year period beginning in June 1959, a study of adolescent street gangs was conducted by a University of Chicago research team in cooperation with the YMCA of Metropolitan Chicago (see Short and Strodtbeck 1965). The purpose of this study was to test recently developed macro-level theories of gang delinquency—Cohen (1955), Cohen and Short (1958), Miller (1958), and Cloward and Ohlin (1960)—by analyzing the individual and collective behavior patterns of gang members. Toward this end, "detached workers" with 12 black and 8 white gangs[8] were asked to report to in regularly scheduled interviews the behaviors, interactions, and activities they had observed or had learned of over the past week (or two) of contact with the gang boys. In addition, graduate students were employed to observe the gangs, nearly always in the company of a detached worker, and to prepare written reports about their field experiences. Altogether, the detached worker interviews and observer field notes produced 16,566 pages of text. Early analyses of these data yielded a number of insights, the most notable of which implicated microsocial factors ("group processes") as key mechanisms leading to the occurrence of violence among gang members (see Short and Strodtbeck 1965).

---

[8] Gangs were initially selected on the basis of their reputation for "trouble," which was determined through police complaints, reports of welfare agencies, and efforts of the detached workers. Later, gangs were selected on the basis of their compatibility with theoretical notions of "delinquent subcultures" (Short and Strodtbeck 1965:78).

The current research revisits these original data and findings. Content analysis of the detached workerr interviews and observer reports is used to address hypotheses derived from impression management theory (see Chapter 6) and to explore interrelationships among microsocial variables and processes associated with incidents that culminate in violent behavior and those that do not (see Chapter 7).

MEASUREMENT

All detached worker interviews and observer reports were read twice and content analyzed using a coding scheme designed to facilitate examination of the influence of microsocial variables in dispute-related incidents (see Appendix A). Application of the coding scheme proceeded as follows.

Dispute-related Incidents

A dispute-related incident was considered to have occurred when an influence attempt/order was met with either rebellious compliance or non-compliance, when an identity attack was made, when one party directly or indirectly attacked or in some way expressed anger at another as a result of some other type of alleged wrongdoing (Felson 1993), when at least one of the parties had a preexisting hostility, or when any type of reciprocal combat (e.g., hand to hand, etc.) developed following a predatory act by one party.[9] For analytical purposes, the initial aggressor—i.e., the first person who became angry or threatened, ordered, reproached, issued an identity attack, physically attacked, or otherwise confronted another—was considered "the offender," regardless of outcome. When there was no clear initial aggressor, three decision rules were applied. First, gang members take precedence over nongang individuals as the offender. Second, members of the gang under observation take precedence as the offender in disputes involving two gangs, unless the member of the second gang was shown to have inflicted more physical damage or demonstrated greater aggression. Third, no one takes precedence as the offender in disputes involving members of the same gang, except for instances when greater aggression or inflicted physical harm is undisputed.

---

[9] Incidents occurring between members of at least two different gangs were considered dispute-related.

Action Types

To the extent permitted by the data, the actions (and targets of the actions) of all parties present during a dispute-related incident were recorded in order of occurrence. Each action was classified into one of the following categories (see Felson 1984:115; Felson and Steadman 1983:62-63):

Norm- or rule-violation: all behaviors that are inappropriate or are perceived to be inappropriate, including "annoying" behavior, failure to fulfill an obligation, ignoring, causing or contributing to another's loss, boasting or "getting bad," cheating, unacceptable demeanor, infidelity, and taking and/or violating another person's property

Reproach: all social control actions that implicate the behavior of their target, including commands to discontinue offensive behavior or to leave, protests, complaints, chastisement, and demands for accounts or redress

Influence attempt/order: all unprovoked actions intended to produce compliance, such as requests or commands made to influence the target to engage in or to not engage in a certain behavior

Compliance: acquiescence to influence attempts/orders, reproaches, etc.

Rebellious compliance: begrudging acquiescence to influence attempts/orders, reproaches, etc.

Noncompliance: explicit or implicit refusal to comply with influence attempts/orders, reproaches, etc.

Identity attacks: all direct attacks on identity, including accusations, insults, non-threatening challenges, physical violations that do not result in bodily harm, and degrading rejections and yelling

Non-weapon threat: weaponless threats that some type of harm will be forthcoming, including verbal challenges and dares, threatening gestures, contingent threats, etc.

Weapon threat: threats backed by a weapon that some type of harm will be forthcoming, including verbal challenges and dares, threatening gestures, contingent threats, etc.

Evasive actions: behaviors that are undertaken to avoid influence attempts/orders, reproaches, identity and physical attacks, or threats without withdrawing/submitting entirely or constituting outright non-compliance, including pleas for help, asking for clarification, etc.

Mediation: all actions undertaken by third parties and/or co-offenders and co-victims to prevent an incident entirely or at least stop it from escalating

Instigation: all actions on the part of third parties and/or co-offenders and co-victims that encourage or otherwise support violent behavior

Accounts/aligning actions: all actions undertaken by the offender or the victim that are meant to explain, excuse, or justify previous or future behavior, including apologies, offering of a hand, etc.

Physical attack: all harmful physical violations, including pursuits undertaken to physically attack another, the use of any kind of weapon, destruction of property, etc.

Submission/withdrawal: all actions undertaken to back down from a dispute, including leaving the scene entirely, fleeing from the antagonist, etc.

Situational Characteristics

Situational characteristics were measured in accordance with their treatment in the literature (see Chapter 2). However, slight adjustments and additions were made for certain measures in order to increase their applicability within the context of adolescent street gangs.

Setting

Setting was measured in two ways. On one hand, location refers to the distinction between public and private spheres of action. A location was considered to be public (coded as 1) if there were few to no restrictions as to whom was allowed to be present. Examples of public locations include amphitheaters, beaches, local gymnasiums, parks, pool halls, open parties, restaurants, taverns, and streets and street corners. Private locations (coded as 0) were more restricted and included such places as houses and apartments (unless it was clear that an "open party" was being held), cars, and gang clubrooms or meeting rooms. On the other hand, territory or "turf" refers to the extent to which the individuals involved in a dispute typically hung out in a particular area. Places where neither party of a dispute typically hung out were coded as 0; places where one party typically hung out were coded as 1; and places where both parties typically hung out were coded as 2.

Offender-victim Relationship

In addition to coding for the specific relationship of the victim to the offender (e.g., 1 = relative, 2 = girlfriend/boyfriend, 3 = gang member friend; 4 = non-gang member friend, 5 = sponsoree, 6 = detached worker/observer, 7 = other authority figure, 8 = rival, 9 = acquaintance; 10 = stranger, 11 = other), a separate measure of the offender-victim gang relationship was constructed. Disputes occurring between members of the same gang were coded as 1 = intra-gang disputes occurring between members of two different gangs were coded as 2 = inter-gang; disputes occurring between a member of a gang against an individual with no known gang affiliation were coded as 3 = extra-group; and disputes occurring between two individuals with no known gang affiliation were coded as 99 = no gang relationship.

Victim Behavior
Aside from examining victim behavior as a possible reason for the occurrence of dispute-related incidents (e.g., norm-violation), two measures of victim behavior following the initial attack by the offender were constructed. Victim resistance, which included all behaviors that challenged the offender but did not involve a physical attack (e.g., non-compliance, threats, identity attacks, etc.), was measured as a dichotomous variable, with 0 = no and 1 = yes. Victim acquiescence, which included such behaviors as apologies and other types of aligning action, was also measured as a dichotomous variable, with 0 = no and 1 = yes.

Detached Workers and Other Third Parties
The presence of detached workers and the presence of third parties were both measured as dichotomous variables (0 = no; 1 = yes). With the exception of detached worker participation (whether as the offender, the victim, or a co-offender or co-victim), which was coded as 3, detached worker behavior and third party behavior also are coded identically. Instigating behavior was coded as 0; bystanding behavior was coded as 1; and protective or mediating behavior was coded as 2. Bystanding third party characteristics was measured as a dichotomous variable, with male youth coded as 1 and all others coded as 0.

Intoxicants
Use of intoxicants was measured as an ordinal variable, with 0 = neither party of the dispute was under the influence of intoxicants, 1 = one party of the dispute was under the influence of intoxicants, and 2 = both parties of the dispute were under the influence of intoxicants. Distinctions were not made between offenders and co-offenders and between victims and co-victims, nor were they made between types of intoxicants.

Weaponry
Weapons possession and weapons threat were both treated as ordinal variables. Each was coded as 0 = neither, 1 = one party, and 2 = both parties. Distinctions were not made between offenders and co-offenders and between victims and co-victims. Distinctions also were not made between weapon types.

Co-offender(s) and Co-victims(s)

Co-offender presence and co-victim presence were each treated as a dichotomous variable, coded 0 = no and 1 = yes. Co-offender behavior and co-victim behavior also were treated as dichotomous variables, coded 0 = no instigating co-offender(s)/no instigating co-victim and 1 = instigating co-offender(s)/instigating co-victim(s).

Dispute Outcome

Dispute outcome was coded dichotomously, with 0 = non-violent and 1 = violent).[10] An incident was coded as non-violent if there was no evidence of a physical attack (e.g., grabbing, pushing, chasing, hitting, or fighting with or without weapons), even though there had been some indication of a desire, intention, likelihood, and/or pressure to engage in violence. Escalation of potentially violent incidents was considered to have occurred when any type of physical attack was initiated.[11]

Within the non-violent category, a distinction was made between "avoided" and "potential." A non-violent incident was treated as avoided if there was no face-to-face interaction between the offender and victim. In potential disputes, on the other hand, an opportunity for a direct confrontation between offenders and victims was present.

ANALYSIS

Quantitative analysis of the data proceeds in two stages. In the first stage, all hypotheses are tested. When reference is made to proportions, univariate frequency and percentage distributions are used. For hypotheses involving associations, however, analyses involve bivariate cross-classifications of dispute outcome (violent v. non-violent) by each one of the predictor variables. In the second stage, emphasis shifts to exploratory analyses of interaction sequences. Action frequencies for

---

[10] Because this general measure of dispute outcome does not distinguish between violence committed by either of the primary disputants (or violence committed by the primary disputants and others), separate measures of physical attack by each of the main disputants were also constructed (0 = no; 1 = yes).

[11] Because detached worker and observer reports frequently indicate only that a "fight" occurred, with no further details concerning the nature of the violence, I do not examine the extent to which findings vary according to differences in level of violence.

each actor are compared for each type of dispute-related incident (all, verbal only, verbal with weapon threat, physical attack without weapon, attempted weapon attack, and weapon attack).[12] Following this, event order is examined by coding each type of action as a proportion of the total number of actions and then computing the mean and standard deviation of each type of action (see Felson 1984; Felson and Steadman 1983). For example, if ten actions occurred during an incident, the first action was coded as 0.1, the second as 0.2, and so on until the final act, which in all cases was coded as 1.0.

Qualitative analysis of the narrative data was also undertaken (see Chapter 7). I read through the full set of detached worker interviews and observer reports twice, comparing and contrasting cases to one another in order to uncover themes related to the independent and joint influence of microsocial factors and processes on the occurrence and unfolding of disputes. I guarded against "anecdotalism" by using the quantitative data as a check on my interpretations (see Silverman, 2001).

Ethnographic data are particularly useful for exploring the dynamic processes of ongoing interaction, most of which are difficult, if not impossible, to capture reliably using data based on verbal or behavioral responses elicited through surveys or laboratory experiments. Note, however, that observations were made of gang boys primarily in leisure activities with their peers; interactions with non-gang individuals at school, work, or at home rarely were observed and generally were learned of only when such information was volunteered by the gang boys themselves.

INTER-CODER RELIABILITY

A random sample of approximately 5% of all dispute-related incidents (n = 167) was coded by another researcher (Coder B) following the presentation of detailed instructions by the original coder. Although it was at times necessary for the original coder to provide clarification of codes and categories and to help locate names on gang rosters, the two coders worked independently of one another. Overall, there is a high

---

[12] Property destruction was not included due to the fact that interaction between offender and victim rarely occurred.

degree of interrater agreement, with Cohen's kappa statistic[13] higher than .70 for the majority of fields (80%) and oftentimes (50%) falling in the .80 to 1.00 range. The coders met afterwards to determine the main source of the discrepancies for those fields having lower kappa values (territory = .318; co-victim behavior toward victim = .611; precedent = .524; victim account = .462; incident serious or non-serious = .619, and offender and victim same race = .533). Differences were accounted for primarily by Coder B's relatively limited familiarity with the gangs, gang members, and their respective neighborhoods, as indicated by a greater use of the "indeterminable" option. In addition, Coder B mistakenly assumed that: (1) individuals who did not belong to a gang could not be linked to a particular territory; (2) co-victims more or less automatically were instigative/supportive when they were present; and (3) no victim account or aligning action (as opposed to indeterminable) was offered if none had been reported. Coder B also used the "indeterminable" option to a slightly greater extent for the field pertaining to the apparent seriousness of an incident. Once these key differences were resolved, the originally low kappa values all increased to above acceptable levels (at least .70).

MISSING DATA PROBLEM

Because the data used in this study were provided by people untrained in observational techniques and were not collected for the purpose of analyzing the importance of the microsocial level in dispute-related incidents, there was widespread variation in their comprehensiveness. While there were over 3,000 incidents extracted from the detached worker and observer reports, complete information was provided for fewer than 5% of cases. Some reports contained information sufficient for coding most variables; others contained data on only one or two and perhaps a couple of others. Missing data was much more extensive for some variables than for others, however. Workers and observers generally reported sufficient information on who was involved in a dispute and where it took place. In contrast, information about

---

[13] "Cohen's kappa measures the agreement between the evaluations of two raters when both are rating the same object. A value of 1 indicates perfect agreement. A value of 0 indicates that agreement is no better than chance" (SPSS for Windows, Rel. 11.0.1. 2001).

intoxicants and weapons rarely was reported, possibly because both were such ordinary features of gang life. In addition, the difficulty of observing and recalling all the steps in an interaction sequence (i.e., who said what and when) certainly contributed to the large amount of missing data for victim behavior. Finally, complete information on *all* audience members (i.e., who was there and how they behaved) was reported infrequently; instead, worker and observer reports of third parties typically discussed the characteristics and behavior of those who were most noticeable and/or with whom they were most familiar.

Because few reports contained data on all of the relevant microsocial factors and processes, taking the traditional approach of excluding cases that are missing on any of the predictor variables would have resulted in a (very small) sample of cases that was not representative of all reported dispute-related incidents. In addition, when the missing data problem is severe (as it is in this study), both the inclusion of categories for whether data are missing for each predictor variable and the use of methods based on value imputation are problematic, with resulting analyses being extraordinarily complicated and unfeasible.

While missing data precluded the implementation of complex statistical modeling in this particular study (but see Hughes and Short 2005 for application of multivariate models to these data), the sheer number of cases and the overlap in the types of information contained therein meant that a sufficient amount of data was available for comparative analyses to be undertaken qualitatively. Such analyses dealt more effectively with cases containing only partial information than did quantitative techniques and thus proved to be of considerable importance.

CHAPTER 6
Quantitative Analyses

INTRODUCTION

Over 3,000 dispute-related incidents (N = 3,505) were extracted from the observer and detached worker reports. Of these incidents, 307 (8.8%) were determined to be non-serious[14] and were removed from the analysis. The results that follow are from univariate and bivariate analyses of the remaining 3,198 incidents, 225 (7.0%) of which were "avoided," 1573 (49.2%) of which were "potential," and 1400 (43.8%) of which were "actual." Bivariate analyses also were conducted with avoided disputes excluded. Findings from these analyses are reported only when they differ from complete-case analyses. In addition, when sufficiently detailed information was provided (N = 268), sequential interactions between the main participants of a dispute were analyzed. Analyses of interaction sequences included an examination of action frequencies and event order.

---

[14] An incident was coded as non-serious when verbal or physical exchanges were reported as being undertaken solely for recreational purposes or fun (e.g., body-punching, kidding, etc.) and/or were observed to be interpreted by participants as play.

BIVARIATE ANALYSES
Hypothesis 1: Setting (Location and Territory)

To determine whether or not most dispute-related incidents were reported to have occurred in public places where both the offender and victim typically hung out, I examined the distribution of disputes by location and by territory, first separately and then in combination. Table 1 shows the distribution of dispute-related incidents by location; Table 2 shows the distribution of such incidents by territory. These data indicate that most disputes emerged in public locations (85.8%) and in places where both the offender and victim typically hung out (72.5%).

Table 1. Dispute-related Incidents by Location

	Frequency	Percent	Cumulative Percent
Private	345	14.2	14.2
Public	2082	85.8	100.0
Subtotal	2427	100.0	
Indeterminable	771		
Total	3198		

Table 2. Dispute-related Incidents by Territory

	Frequency	Percent	Cumulative Percent
Neither Party's	29	1.8	1.8
One Party's	406	25.6	27.5
Both Parties'	1148	72.5	100.0
Subtotal	1583	100.0	
Indeterminable	1615		
Total	3198		

When location and territory are combined (Table 3), the order of proportions generally is as expected. Dispute-related incidents that occurred in public places where both the offender and victim hung out comprise the largest category (57.6%), followed by dispute-related incidents that occurred in public places where only one party hung out (19.1%). Not surprisingly, a greater proportion of dispute-related incidents occurred in private locations where both the offender and victim hung out (18.7%) than in public locations where neither party hung out (1.6%). This finding can be attributed to the greater amount of time spent by gang members in their own turf than in less familiar territory.

Table 3. Dispute-related Incidents by Location and Territory Combined

Location	Territory			Total
	Neither Party's	One Party's	Both Parties'	
Private	4 (.3%)	38 (2.7%)	265 (18.7%)	307 (21.7%)
Public	23 (1.6%)	270 (19.1%)	816 (57.6%)	1109 (78.3%)
Total	27 (1.9%)	308 (21.8%)	1081 (76.3%)	1416 (100.0)%

Disputes that occurred within the territory of one party but not the other were hypothesized to be more likely than disputes that occurred in more neutral territories to escalate into violence. The rationale is that status concerns are greatest for gangs and for gang members when turf claims are at stake. Table 4 presents data on dispute outcome by territory. As expected, these data indicate that dispute-related incidents were most likely to result in violence when they occurred in the territory of one party but not the other (Somers' d_{yx} = .174).[15] When neither party of a potentially violent dispute had a more legitimate claim to territory, a non-violent resolution was more likely. However, it is important to note that this finding does not take into consideration the offender-victim relationship, which qualitative analysis of the data reveals to be of great consequence.

Table 4. Dispute Outcome by Territory

Dispute Outcome	Territory		Total
	Neutral (Neither or Both)	One Party's	
Non-violent	811 (68.9%)	209 (51.5%)	1020 (64.4%)
Violent	366 (31.1%)	197 (48.5%)	563 (35.6%)
Total	1177 (100.0%)	406 (100.0%)	1583 (100.0%)

χ^2 = 40.002; df = 1; p < .001
Somers' d_{yx} = .174

Together, these findings suggest that, although dispute-related incidents were most likely to occur in public places where both the offender and victim typically hung out, dispute outcome depended more on the extent to which territorial rights were at stake. Consistent with Hypothesis 1, disputes that occurred in the territory of one party but not the other were more likely than disputes that occurred in more neutral territories to escalate into violence.

---

[15] Results remain essentially unchanged when all incidents in which there was some (known) preexisting hostility between disputants are excluded from the analysis, and the strength of the relationship increases considerably (Somers' d_{yx} = .267) when avoided disputes are removed from the analysis.

Hypothesis 2: Offender-Victim Relationship

Miller et al. (1961) found that aggressive actions among members of the adolescent street corner group they studied were most often intra-gang (70.4%), a finding attributed largely to interaction frequency. These Chicago gang data provide a slight contrast. Table 5 shows the distribution of dispute-related incidents by offender-victim relationship. Disputes were most likely to occur between a gang member and an individual with no known gang affiliation (37.6%), followed by inter-gang member disputes (25.7%). Disputes between two members of the same gang were less common (17.7%). It is clear, however, that many of the extra-group disputes involved individuals with whom the relevant gang member was likely to be in frequent interaction and thus with whom there were numerous opportunities for conflict (e.g., detached worker, other authority figure, relative or acquaintance).

Table 5. Dispute-related Incidents by Offender-victim Relationship

	Frequency	Percent of Total (N = 3198)*
Intra-gang	567	17.7
Relative	12	0.4
Gang Member Friend	555	17.4
Inter-gang	822	25.7
Relative	1	0.0
Boyfriend/Girlfriend	3	0.1
Gang member friend	121	3.8
Rival	597	18.7
Stranger	2	0.1
Indeterminable	98	3.1

Table 5 continued. Dispute-related Incidents by Offender-victim Relationship

	Frequency	Percent of Total (N = 3198)
Extra-group	1201	37.6
Relative	66	2.1
Boyfriend/Girlfriend	53	1.7
Gang member friend	19	0.6
Non-gang member friend	28	0.9
Sponsoree	213	6.7
Detached worker/Observer	112	3.5
Other authority figure	116	3.6
Rival	11	0.3
Acquaintance	119	3.7
Stranger	133	4.2
Other	250	4.7
Indeterminable	181	5.7
No Gang	174	5.4
Relative	9	0.3
Boyfriend/Girlfriend	7	0.2
Non-gang member friend	14	0.4
Sponsoree	1	0.0
Other authority figure	18	0.6
Rival	1	0.0
Acquaintance	19	0.6
Stranger	26	0.8
Other	36	1.1
Indeterminable	43	1.3

Table 5 continued. Dispute-related Incidents by Offender-victim Relationship

	Frequency	Percent of Total (N = 3198)
Indeterminable Gang	434	13.6
Relative	4	0.1
Boyfriend/Girlfriend	4	0.1
Gang member friend	1	0.0
Other Authority	3	0.1
Rival	2	0.1
Acquaintance	3	0.1
Stranger	10	0.3
Other	8	0.3
Indeterminable	349	12.5

*In order to minimize loss of information provided in those cases in which the specific offender-victim relationship was known but the offender-victim gang relationship was unknown or vice versa, the "indeterminable" category is included in calculations of percentages.

Although dispute-related incidents were most likely to involve a gang member and an individual with no known gang affiliation, such incidents were not the most likely to escalate into violence. As shown in Table 6, which presents data on dispute outcome by offender-victim gang relationship, violent outcomes were more common for disputes that emerged between members of different gangs (54.7%) than for disputes involving any other type of offender-victim gang relationship (31.6 – 36.0%). These data do not differentiate between rival and friendly gangs, however.

Table 6. Dispute Outcome by Offender-Victim Gang Relationship

| | Offender-victim Gang Relationship | | | | Total |
	Intra-	Inter-	Extra-	No Gang	
Non-violent	363 (64.0%)	372 (45.3%)	776 (64.6%)	119 (68.4%)	1630 (59.0%)
Violent	204 (36.0%)	450 (54.7%)	425 (35.4%)	55 (31.6%)	1134 (41.0%)
Total	567 (100.0%)	822 (100.0%)	1201 (100.0%)	174 (100.0%)	2764 (100.0%)

$\chi^2 = 92.069$; df = 3; p < .001
C = .180; Φ = .183; Lambda = .069

Table 7 presents data on dispute outcome by offender-victim gang relationship, comparing disputes between rival gang members with disputes involving all other types of offender-victim gang relationships combined. Because individual status concerns are compounded by added social pressure to defend or extend existing gang status when disputes emerge between members of rival gangs, impression management theory leads to the prediction that these disputes will be the most likely to escalate into violence. In support, there is a significant, positive relationship between offender-victim gang relationship and dispute outcome (Somers' d_{yx} = .235).[16] The strength of this relationship increases (Somers' d_{yx} = .262) when all incidents in which there was a known history of antagonism between individual

---

[16] The strength of the relationship between offender-victim gang relationship and dispute outcome increases considerably when avoided disputes are excluded from the analysis (Somers' d_{yx} = .328).

disputants are removed from the analysis (data not presented). Thus, the finding that violence is especially likely in disputes between members of rival gangs cannot be accounted for solely by preexisting hostilities; immediate factors related to the offender-victim relationship appear to be important.

Table 7. Dispute Outcome by Offender-victim Gang Relationship (Rival Gang Member v. Else)

| Dispute Outcome | Rival Gang Member | | Total |
	No	Yes	
Non-violent	1349 (64.2%)	243 (40.7%)	1592 (59.0%)
Violent	753 (35.8%)	354 (59.3%)	1107 (41.0%)
Total	2102 (100.0%)	597 (100.0%)	2699 (100.0%)

$\chi^2 = 105.894$; df = 1; p < .001
Somers' d_{yx} = .235

Overall, Hypothesis 2 is supported by these data. Dispute-related incidents occurred most often between a gang member and an individual with no known gang affiliation. As predicted, however, disputes involving the greatest status concerns—that is, rival gang disputes—were the most likely to escalate into violence.

Hypotheses 3a, 3b, and 3c: Victim Behavior
On the basis of impression management theory, I hypothesized that victims would be found to have played a key role in the occurrence and outcome of dispute-related incidents. The data indicate that victim behavior was, in fact, important to both. Table 8, which presents data on the reason for dispute occurrence, shows that the greatest proportion

of all disputes emerged as a result of the victim engaging in a norm-violation or not complying with an order issued by the offender (38.9%). Unprovoked identity attacks by the offender occurred less than half as often (16.0%). Thus, it was not uncommon for victims to initiate disputes (intentionally or unintentionally) through words and/or actions that upset the offender.

Table 8. Dispute-related Incidents by Reason for Occurrence

	Frequency	Percent	Cumulative Percent
Rule- or Order-violation	939	38.9	38.9
Revenge/Retaliation	660	27.3	66.2
Identity Attack	387	16.0	82.2
Defense of Others	107	4.4	86.6
Jealousy/Competition Opp. Sex	72	3.0	89.6
Unfair/Rough Play	53	2.2	91.8
Territory/Neighborhood Honor	50	2.1	93.9
Money/Debts	39	1.6	95.5
Misunderstanding	38	1.6	97.1
Fun/Recreation	34	1.4	98.5
Other	19	0.8	99.3
Rumors	11	0.5	99.8
General Troublemaking	4	0.2	100.0
Racial Concerns	2	0.1	100.1
Robbery	1	0.0	100.1*
Subtotal	2416	100.0	
Indeterminable	1615		
Total	3198		

*Figures do not total to 100.0% due to rounding.

Table 9 presents data on dispute outcome, measured in terms of whether or not the offender engaged in a physical attack, by victim resistance.[17] These data indicate that violence was slightly more likely to occur when the victim did not challenge the offender than when the offender was faced with opposition from the victim (Somers' d_{yx} = -.087).[18] Although this finding provides evidence of the importance of victim behavior, it contradicts the claim that victim resistance contributes to the escalation of disputes into violence because of the threat that this type of behavior poses to the offender's situated identity. However, it is possible that, following initial resistance, actions taken by the victim (e.g., accounts and aligning action) and/or third parties (e.g., mediation)—both of which are associated with a significant reduction in violence (see below)—may have counteracted the impact of any altercasting that victim resistance had given rise to beforehand.

Table 9. Dispute Outcome (Offender Physical Attack) by Victim Resistance

Dispute Outcome	Victim Resistance		Total
	No	Yes	
Non-violent	347 (70.1%)	631 (78.8%)	980 (75.4%)
Violent	149 (29.9%)	170 (21.2%)	319 (24.6%)
Total	498 (100.0%)	801 (100.0%)	1299 (100.0%)

χ^2 = 12.535; df = 1; p < .001
Somers' d_{yx} = -.087

---

[17] Incidents in which the victim is the first to engage in a physical attack (n = 126) were excluded from the analysis.
[18] The relationship between victim resistance and offender physical attack is no longer significant when analysis is limited to cases in which there was no known precedent (χ^2 = 3.740; df = 1; p = .053; not significant).

To further assess the role of victim behavior in the unfolding of disputes, I examined the distribution of dispute outcome, measured in terms of whether or not the offender engaged in a physical attack, by victim account/aligning action (Table 10). These data show that the provision of an account or other aligning action on the part of the victim significantly increased the likelihood of potential disputes being squashed (Somers' d_{yx} = -.193).[19] Thus, victims who acquiesced to the offender reduced their risk of being physically attacked.

Table 10. Dispute Outcome (Offender Physical Attack) by Victim Account/Aligning Action

Dispute Outcome	Victim Account/Aligning Action		Total
	No	Yes	
Non-violent	597 (68.2%)	334 (87.4%)	931 (74.0%)
Violent	279 (31.8%)	48 (12.6%)	327 (26.0%)
Total	876 (100.0%)	382 (100.0%)	1258 (100.0%)

χ^2 = 51.421; df = 1; p < .001
Somers' d_{yx} = -.193

---

[19] The strength of this relationship decreases slightly when incidents with a known precedent (i.e., preexisting hostility between disputants) are excluded from the analysis (Somers' d_{yx} = -.160).

In sum, results are mixed. In support of Hypotheses 3a and 3c, the data indicate that victim behavior oftentimes was an important factor in the occurrence of dispute-related incidents and that victim acquiescence was associated with the development of non-violent dispute outcomes. Contrary to Hypothesis 3b, the data also show that the likelihood of violence was not enhanced by victim resistance; rather, disputes were more likely to be resolved violently when the victim did not challenge the offender than when the victim did. As noted above, however, caution must be exercised when interpreting this finding, as it does not take into account actions taken by the victim and/or audience members following the initial resistance.

Hypothesis 4: Detached Worker and Third Parties
To determine the importance of the external audience in dispute-related incidents, I first examined frequency and percentage distributions of third party, detached worker, and observer presence and behavior. I then examined the effect of detached worker and third party behavior on dispute outcome.

Table 11 shows the distribution of dispute-related incidents by third party presence. These data indicate that, of those cases for which there was sufficient information, third parties were present in 97.5% of the cases. When information on the presence of a non-participating detached worker (53.9% of all cases) and non-participating observer (13.1% of all cases) is included (Table 12),[20] this figure increases to 98.9%. Within the observed context, then, there was a strong tendency for disputes to emerge in front of an external audience. This is consistent with Hypothesis 4a.

---

[20] Incidents in which the detached worker participated as an offender, victim, co-offender, or co-victim (N = 429) were not included in calculation of detached worker presence. Similarly, calculation of observer presence did not include participating observers (N = 17).

Table 11. Dispute-related Incidents by Presence of Third Parties

	Frequency	Percent	Cumulative Percent
No Third Parties	47	2.5	2.5
Third Parties Present	1807	97.5	100.0
Subtotal	1854	100.0	
Indeterminable	1344		
Total	3198		

Table 12. Dispute-related Incidents by Presence of Non-participating Detached Worker (DW), Non-participating Observer (OBS), and Third Parties (TP)

	Frequency	Percent	Cumulative Percent
No DW, OBS, or TP	24	1.1	1.1
DW, OBS, and/or TP	2166	98.9	100.0
Subtotal	2190	100.0	
Indeterminable	1008		
Total	3198		

Table 13 presents data on the frequency and percentage distributions of detached worker, observer, and third party behavior. When detached workers were not actively participating in a dispute-related incident (27.1%), they were most likely to mediate (39.6%) or act as a bystander (32.3%) and almost never engaged in protective (0.1%) or instigating behavior (0.8%). Observers, of course, were most likely to act as a bystander (96.0%). Similar to detached workers, third parties were most likely to mediate (37.4%) or act as a bystander (56.5%); protective (0.5%) and instigating (5.6%) behaviors were rare.

Table 13. Dispute-related Incidents by Detached Worker, Observer, and Third Party Behavior

	Frequency	Percent	Cumulative Percent
Detached Worker			
Protective	2	0.1	0.1
Instigating	13	0.8	0.9
Mediating	627	39.6	40.6
Bystanding	512	32.3	72.9
Participating	429	27.1	100.0
Subtotal	1583	100.0	
Indeterminable	159		
Not Present/Indeterminable	1456		
Total	3198		
Observer			
Protective	0	0.0	0.0
Instigating	0	0.0	0.0
Mediating	0	0.0	0.0
Bystanding	411	96.0	96.0
Participating	17	4.0	100.0
Subtotal	428	100.0	
Indeterminable	1		
Not Present/Indeterminable	2769		
Total	3198		
Third Party			
Protective	8	0.5	0.5
Instigating	82	5.6	6.2
Mediating	546	37.4	43.5
Bystanding	825	56.5	100.0
Subtotal	1461	100.0	
Indeterminable	346		
Not Present/Indeterminable	1391		
Total	3198		

Table 14 shows the distribution of dispute outcome by detached worker presence. These data indicate a strong, negative relationship (Somers' d_{yx} = -.473), meaning the mere presence of a detached worker—regardless of his behavior—reduced the likelihood of violence.[21]

Table 14. Dispute Outcome by Detached Worker Presence

| Dispute Outcome | Detached Worker Presence | | Total |
	No	Yes	
Non-violent	338 (30.2%)	1350 (77.5%)	1688 (59.0%)
Violent	783 (69.8%)	392 (22.5%)	1175 (41.0%)
Total	1121 (100.0%)	1742 (100.0%)	2863 (100.0%)

χ^2 = 631.861; df = 1; p < .001
Somers' d_{yx} = -.473

Table 15 presents data on the distribution of dispute outcome by third party presence. These data indicate that the mere presence of third parties, regardless of their behavior, significantly increased the likelihood of violent dispute outcomes (Somers' d_{yx} = .249).

---

[21] When incidents involving a participating detached worker are removed from the analysis, the strength of this relationship decreases but nevertheless remains significant and strong (Somers' d_{yx} = -.430).

Table 15. Dispute Outcome by Third Party Presence

	Third Party Presence		
Dispute Outcome	No	Yes	Total
Non-violent	41 (87.2%)	1127 (62.4%)	1168 (63.0%)
Violent	6 (12.8%)	680 (37.6%)	686 (37.0%)
Total	47 (100.0%)	1807 (100.0%)	1854 (100.0%)

$\chi^2 = 12.150$; df = 1; p < .001
Somers' $d_{yx} = .249$

Table 16 shows the distribution of dispute outcome by detached worker behavior for all cases that emerged in the presence of a worker whose behavior was discernable and non-participatory. These data indicate that there is no relationship between detached worker behavior and dispute outcome ($\chi^2 = 2.586$; df = 2; p = 2.586; not significant). This finding is contrary to Hypothesis 4b.

Table 16. Dispute Outcome by Detached Worker Behavior

	Detached Worker Behavior			
Dispute Outcome	Instigating	Bystanding	Protecting/ Mediating	Total
Non-violent	9 (69.2%)	386 (75.4%)	448 (71.2%)	843 (73.1%)
Violent	4 (30.8%)	126 (24.6%)	181 (28.8%)	311 (26.9%)
Total	13 (100.0%)	512 (100.0%)	629 (100.0%)	1154 (100.0%)

$\chi^2 = 2.586$; df = 2; p = .274
Somers' $d_{yx} = .038$

Data on the distribution of dispute outcome by third party behavior for all cases that emerged in front of third parties whose behavior was discernable (Table 17) also are contrary to Hypothesis 4b. These data indicate that there is a significant but weak, positive relationship between third party behavior and dispute outcome (Somers' d_{yx} = .093), suggesting that violence was slightly more likely to develop when third parties mediated/protected and slightly less likely to develop when they instigated.

Table 17. Dispute Outcome by Third Party Behavior

Dispute Outcome	Third Party Behavior			Total
	Instigating	Bystanding	Protecting/ Mediating	
Non-violent	48 (58.5%)	576 (69.8%)	314 (56.7%)	938 (64.2%)
Violent	34 (41.5%)	249 (30.2%)	240 (43.3%)	523 (35.8%)
Total	82 (100.0%)	825 (100.0%)	554 (100.0%)	1461 (100.0%)

χ^2 = 26.111; df = 2; p < .001
Somers' d_{yx} = .093

Findings presented above may be misleading in that they include all cases involving detached worker or third party mediation, regardless of the point at which such behavior took place in the overall interaction sequence. To adjust for the problem of temporal order, I removed from analysis those cases in which mediation occurred after physical attack (n = 290) and then reexamined the effect of detached worker behavior and third party behavior on dispute outcome (Table 18 and Table 19, respectively). These data reveal a significant, negative relationship between dispute outcome and both third party behavior (Somers' d_{yx} = -.139) and detached worker behavior (Somers' d_{yx} = -.149). Thus, when third parties and detached workers engaged in instigative behavior, the likelihood of a violent dispute outcome increased. Mediating/protective behavior, on the other hand, increased the likelihood that a dispute would be resolved non-violently.

Table 18. Dispute Outcome by Detached Worker Behavior (Mediation After Violence Cases Excluded)

| Dispute Outcome | Detached Worker Behavior | | | Total |
	Instigating	Bystanding	Protecting/ Mediating	
Non-violent	9 (75.0%)	386 (79.1%)	448 (93.1%)	843 (85.9%)
Violent	3 (25.0%)	102 (20.9%)	33 (6.9%)	138 (14.1%)
Total	12 (100.0%)	488 (100.0%)	481 (100.0%)	981 (100.0%)

$\chi^2 = 40.707$; df = 2; p < .001
Somers' $d_{yx} = -.139$

Table 19. Dispute Outcome by Third Party Behavior (Mediation After Violence Cases Excluded)

| Dispute Outcome | Third Party Behavior | | | Total |
	Instigating	Bystanding	Protecting/ Mediating	
Non-violent	48 (64.9%)	576 (73.7%)	314 (89.0%)	938 (77.6%)
Violent	26 (35.1%)	206 (26.3%)	39 (11.0%)	271 (22.4%)
Total	74 (100.0%)	782 (100.0%)	353 (100.0%)	1209 (100.0%)

$\chi^2 = 40.048$; df = 2; p < .001
Somers' $d_{yx} = -.149$

Subsequent analyses comparing the impact of mediating behavior by detached workers and third parties on all disputes, including those that did not occur in the presence of an external audience, revealed an even stronger relationship between dispute outcome and mediating detached worker (Somers' d_{yx} = -.453) and produced similar results for mediating third parties (Somers' d_{yx} = -.152).[22] In support of Hypothesis 4b, then, the unfolding of disputes clearly was influenced by audience behavior.

In contrast, the effect of bystanding third parties on dispute outcome did not vary as predicted (Table 20). Although the likelihood of a violent dispute outcome was shown in data not presented to be significantly higher when bystanders were present than when there were no third parties (χ^2 = 6.518; df = 1; p < .05; Somers' d_{yx} = .174), Table 20 shows that there is a significant, negative relationship between the characteristics of bystanders and dispute outcome (Somers' d_{yx} = -.119). Thus, non-violent dispute outcomes were more likely when the non-active audience of a dispute consisted primarily of male youth than when other types of people (e.g., adults, female peers, and young children) were watching.[23] This finding remains unchanged when analysis is limited to those disputes in which at least one participant was known to be an active gang member or in which no non-participating detached worker was present (data not presented). However, the relationship between bystanding male youth and dispute outcome loses its significance when all cases in which a detached worker was present are excluded from the analysis. This suggests the possibility that detached worker presence may have been a more important situational cue than was the presence of other types of

---

[22] Corresponding analyses of the impact of instigative behavior were not conducted because of the rarity of such behavior.

[23] When youth, whether male or female, are compared to all other categories of bystanding third parties, the relationship between bystanding third parties and dispute outcome loses its significance (χ^2 = 3.281; df = 1; p = .070; not significant). Interestingly, however, a significant, positive relationship emerges when bystanding female youth are compared to all other categories of bystanding third parties (Somers' d_{yx} = .171), meaning the likelihood of a violent dispute outcome was higher when the audience consisted primarily of female peers than when there were other types of bystanding audience members. Note, however, the bystanding audience was made up of female peers only in a small number of cases (n = 37).

bystanders. It could also be that male youth bystanders were perceived as being unfavorable toward violence when their detached worker was involved in a dispute. Regardless of the reason, however, these data are contrary to Hypothesis 4c. Individuals involved in potentially violent disputes apparently did not impute pro-violent values to bystanding male youth. If they did, their behavior did not reflect it.

Table 20. Dispute Outcome by Characteristics of Bystanding Third Parties

Dispute Outcome	Male Youth		Total
	Yes	No	
Non-violent	71 (60.2%)	493 (72.1%)	564 (70.3%)
Violent	47 (39.8%)	191 (27.9%)	238 (29.7%)
Total	118 (100.0%)	684 (100.0%)	802 (100.0%)

$\chi^2 = 6.836$; df = 1; p < .01
Somers' $d_{yx} = -.119$

Although no evidence is found of a linkage between violence and bystanding male youth, findings generally are consistent with the claim that impression management in front of an external audience is an important concern for individuals who are involved in a dispute. Most dispute-related incidents emerged in the presence of an external audience, and audience behavior was a strong predictor of dispute outcome. When detached workers or third parties instigated, the likelihood of potentially violent disputes escalating into actual violence increased, perhaps as a result of the added pressure that this type of behavior placed on the offender and/or victim to fight for their honor. However, when detached workers or third parties mediated/protected, non-violent dispute outcomes were more likely. Such behavior may have conveyed the message that members of the audience are unfavorable toward violence and that backing down will not result in a loss of face.

Hypothesis 5: Intoxicants

Use of intoxicants—most often alcohol—was ubiquitous among gang boys and often was involved in disputes. Table 21 presents the frequency and percentage distribution of dispute-related incidents by use of intoxicants. Eliminating incidents in which only third parties were under the influence of an intoxicant (n = 90) or in which the use of intoxicants was indeterminable (n = 2325),[24] intoxicants were reported to be influencing neither party in 2.7% (n = 21) of the cases, one party only in 77.3% (n = 605) of the cases, and both parties in 20.1% (n = 157) of the cases.

Table 21. Dispute-related Incidents by Use of Intoxicants

	Frequency	Percent	Cumulative Percent
Neither Party	21	2.7	2.7
One Party Only	605	77.3	79.9
Both Parties	157	20.1	100.0
Subtotal	783	100.0	
Third Party Only	90		
Indeterminable	2325		
Total	3198		

To determine the effect of intoxicants on the unfolding of disputes, I examined the distribution of dispute outcome by reported use of intoxicants (Table 22). These data show that the relationship between dispute outcome and use of intoxicants is significant (χ^2 = 8.143; df = 2; p < .05) and positive (Somers' d_{yx} = .116). [25] Thus, the likelihood of dispute escalation increased as the number of parties under the influence of some kind of intoxicant increased. When intoxicants were absent, a non-violent resolution was more likely.

---

[24] Note that the missing data problem is particularly severe for intoxicants. See Chapter 4 for a likely explanation.

[25] This finding remains unchanged when use of intoxicants among co-offenders and co-victims is not considered (Somers' d_{yx} = .126).

Table 22. Dispute Outcome by Use of Intoxicants

Dispute Outcome	Use of Intoxicants			Total
	Neither Party	One Party	Both Parties	
Non-violent	15 (71.4%)	370 (61.2%)	78 (49.7%)	463 (59.1%)
Violent	6 (28.6%)	235 (38.8%)	79 (50.3%)	320 (40.9%)
Total	21 (100.0%)	605 (100.0%)	157 (100.0%)	783 (100.0%)

$\chi^2 = 8.143$; df = 2; p < .05
Somers' $d_{yx} = .116$

Although Table 23 shows that elimination of avoided disputes from the analysis reduces the relationship between use of intoxicants and dispute outcome to non-significance ($\chi^2 = 5.712$; df = 2; p = .057; not significant), the direction of the relationship remains unchanged (Somers' $d_{yx} = .101$). Closer examination reveals that the change in chi-square can be attributed primarily to 40 avoided disputes in which only one party was known to be under the influence of an intoxicant.

Table 23. Dispute Outcome by Use of Intoxicants (Avoided Dispute-related Incidents Excluded)

Dispute Outcome	Use of Intoxicants			Total
	Neither Party	One Party	Both Parties	
Non-violent	12 (66.7%)	330 (58.4%)	74 (48.4%)	416 (56.5%)
Violent	6 (33.3%)	235 (41.6%)	79 (51.6%)	320 (43.5%)
Total	18 (100.0%)	565 (100.0%)	153 (100.0%)	736 (100.0%)

$\chi^2 = 5.712$; df = 2; p = .057
Somers' $d_{yx} = .101$

Taken together, these data offer some support for Hypothesis 5, which predicted that use of intoxicants would be associated with violence because of the adverse effects that intoxicants typically have on human behavior and social interaction. Such effects include: (1) a predisposition toward socially unacceptable behavior; (2) a proclivity to perceive others' behavior as socially unacceptable even when, in fact, it is not; (3) a heightened intolerance of behavior that is perceived to be or actually is socially unacceptable; and (4) a decreased willingness and/or ability to respond non-violently to the (real or perceived) transgressions on the part of others.

Hypothesis 6: Weapons[26]

Weapons were predicted to play a critical role in the unfolding of disputes. More specifically, I hypothesized that violent outcomes would be associated with weapons on both sides of a dispute, whereas non-violent outcomes would be associated with weapons on only one side of a dispute. To assess the role of weapons, I examined the relationship between dispute outcome and both weapon possession and weapon threat. Data on the distribution of dispute outcome by weapon possession (Table 24) reveal a significant, positive relationship (Somers' d_{yx} = .102). Thus, the likelihood of violence increased as the number of parties to a dispute in possession of a weapon increased. Note, however, that this relationship loses its significance when disputes involving a retaliation motive are excluded from the analysis (χ^2 = 4.957; df = 2; p = .084; not significant). The importance of preexisting hostility in disputes involving weapons is discussed in greater detail when findings from qualitative analysis of the data are presented.

---

[26] **Possession:** Eliminating incidents in which only the third party was reported to be in possession of a weapon (n = 74) or in which the possession of weaponry was indeterminable (n = 2321), weapons were reported to be possessed by neither party in 2.7% (n = 22) of the cases, by one party only in 81.1% (n = 651) of the cases, and by both parties in 16.2% (n = 130) of the cases. **Threat:** Eliminating incidents in which only the third party was reported to have engaged in a weapon threat (n = 20) or in which the threatened use of weaponry was indeterminable (n = 815), at least one weapon threat was reportedly issued by neither party in 89.1% (n = 2105) of the cases, by one party only in 9.2% (n = 217) of the cases, and by both parties in 1.7% (n = 41) of the cases.

Table 24. Dispute Outcome by Possession of Weaponry

Dispute Outcome	Possession of Weaponry			
	Neither Party	One Party	Both Parties	Total
Non-violent	12 (54.5%)	246 (37.8%)	38 (29.2%)	296 (36.9%)
Violent	10 (45.5%)	405 (62.6%)	92 (70.8%)	507 (63.1%)
Total	22 (100.0%)	651 (100.0%)	130 (100.0%)	803 (100.0%)

$\chi^2 = 6.449$; df = 2; p < .05
Somers' $d_{yx} = .102$

Table 25 presents data on the distribution of dispute outcome by weapon threat. These data indicate that the relationship between dispute outcome and weapon threat is also significant and positive (Somers' d_{yx} = .268).[27] Thus, the likelihood of violence increased as the number of parties to a dispute that issued a weapon threat increased.

---

[27] Since findings do not depend on whether or not the target of a weapon threat is armed (data not presented), figures presented here include weapon threats directed at both armed and unarmed parties.

Table 25. Dispute Outcome by Weapon Threat

Dispute Outcome	Weapon Threat			Total
	Neither Party	One Party	Both Parties	
Non-violent	1517 (72.1%)	100 (46.1%)	16 (39.0%)	1633 (69.1%)
Violent	588 (27.9%)	117 (53.9%)	25 (61.0%)	730 (30.9%)
Total	2105 (100.0%)	217 (100.0%)	41 (100.0%)	2363 (100.0%)

$\chi^2 = 79.897$; df = 2; p < .001
Somers' d_{yx} = .268

Findings presented above are consistent with the prediction that disputes in which both parties possessed weaponry and/or engaged in a weapon threat were likely to escalate into violence. However, inspection of the data reveals that neither the possession nor threatened use of weaponry by only one party produced a substantial reduction in the likelihood of a violent dispute outcome. This is demonstrated more clearly in Tables 26 and 27. Table 26 presents data on the effect of weapon possession by only one party compared to the combined effect of weapon possession by neither party or by both parties. These data provide no evidence of a link between non-violent dispute outcomes and possession of weaponry by only one party ($\chi^2 = 1.268$; df = 1; p = .260; not significant). In Table 27, I conduct a similar analysis with weapon threat, comparing the effect of a weapon threat issued by only one party to the combined effect of a weapon threat issued by neither party or by both parties. Results show that a weapon threat by only one party is associated with a significant increase in the likelihood of a violent dispute outcome (Somers' d_{yx} = .254).[28]

---

[28] Further analysis (data not presented) reveals that the effect on dispute outcome of a weapon threat issued by only one party does not differ significantly from the effect of a weapon threat issued by both parties (χ^2 = .694; df = 1; p = .405; not significant).

Table 26. Dispute Outcome by Possession of Weaponry (One Party v. Neither Party and Both Parties)

Dispute Outcome	Possession of Weaponry		
	Neither Party/ Both Parties	One Party	Total
Non-violent	50 (32.9%)	246 (37.8%)	296 (36.9%)
Violent	102 (67.1%)	405 (62.2%)	507 (63.1%)
Total	152 (100.0%)	651 (100.0%)	803 (100.0%)

$\chi^2 = 1.268$; df = 1; p = .260
Somers' d_{yx} = -.049

Table 27. Dispute Outcome by Weapon Threat (One Party v. Neither Party and Both Parties)

Dispute Outcome	Weapon Threat		
	Neither Party/ Both Parties	One Party	Total
Non-violent	1533 (71.4%)	100 (46.1%)	1633 (69.1%)
Violent	613 (28.6%)	117 (53.9%)	730 (30.9%)
Total	2146 (100.0%)	217 (100.0%)	2363 (100.0%)

$\chi^2 = 59.331$; df = 1; p < .001
Somers' d_{yx} = .254

Overall, findings suggest that the likelihood of a dispute escalating into violence increases with the introduction of weapons, regardless of whether it is done by only one party or by both parties.[29] This supports the prediction that weapons on both sides of a dispute would increase the stakes of a character contest to such an extent that neither party would be likely to back down. However, it contradicts the prediction that a weapons imbalance would increase the likelihood of a non-violent dispute outcome primarily because of the opportunity it provides to the unfairly disadvantaged party to back down without suffering a loss of face.

---

[29] Subsequent analyses (data not presented) confirm the role of weapon threat as a predictor of—rather than a response to—violence, showing that weapon threats by one or both parties are significantly related to violence even when those threats that took place after a physical attack are removed from the analysis (Somers' $d_{yx} = .146$ for one party v. neither party; Somers' $d_{yx} = .205$ for both parties v. neither party).

Hypothesis 7: Co-offenders and Co-victims

Table 28 shows the frequency and percentage distribution of co-offender and co-victim presence during dispute-related incidents. When sufficient information was provided, co-offenders and co-victims were shown to have been present in approximately equal proportions (40.1% and 36.2%, respectively).

Table 28. Dispute-related Incidents by Co-offender and Co-victim Presence

	Frequency	Percent	Cumulative Percent
Co-offender(s)			
Not Present	1786	59.9	59.9
Present	1194	40.1	100.0
Subtotal	2980	100.0	
Indeterminable	218		
Total	3198		
Co-victim(s)			
Not Present	1872	63.8	63.8
Present	1063	36.2	100.0
Subtotal	2935	100.0	
Indeterminable	263		
Total	3198		

Their behavior evidenced a great deal of similarity as well (Table 29), with both co-offenders and co-victims being most likely to engage in instigating behavior (96.6% and 72.5%, respectively). However, co-victims tended also to engage in a considerable amount of bystanding (26.5%).[30]

---

[30] Sufficient information on co-offender behavior was provided in 88.6% of the cases, whereas sufficient information on co-victim behavior was provided in only 46.2% of the cases.

Table 29. Dispute-related Incidents by Co-offender and Co-victim Behavior

	Frequency	Percent	Cumulative Percent
Co-offender			
Instigating/Supportive	1022	96.6	96.6
Bystanding	17	1.6	98.2
Mediating	19	1.8	100.0
Subtotal	1058	100.0	
Indeterminable	136		
Not Present	2004		
Total	3198		
Co-victim			
Instigating/Supportive	356	72.5	72.5
Bystanding	130	26.5	99.0
Mediating	5	1.0	100.0
Subtotal	491	100.0	
Indeterminable	572		
Not Present	2135		
Total	3198		

The presence of co-offenders and the behavior of both co-offenders and co-victims were hypothesized to have important implications for the unfolding of disputes. To determine the role of co-offenders and co-victims, I examined the distribution of dispute outcome by co-offender and co-victim presence and by presence of instigating co-offenders and co-victims. Table 30 and Table 31 show the distribution of dispute outcome by presence of co-offenders and by presence of co-victims, respectively.[31] In support of Hypothesis 7a, there is a significant, positive relationship between co-offender presence and dispute outcome (Somers' d_{yx} = .128), meaning offenders

---

[31] Violent incidents included in analyses of the impact of co-offenders and co-victims are limited to those in which only the offender and victim, respectively, engaged in physical attack.

were more likely to engage in physical attack when they entered into a dispute accompanied by others than when they were alone. The strength of this relationship increases considerably when avoided disputes are removed from the analysis (Somers' d_{yx} = .194). Although the presence of co-victims initially is shown to be only weakly related to dispute outcome (Somers' d_{yx} = .070), the strength of this relationship also increases when avoided disputes are removed from the analysis (Somers' d_{yx} = .111). The likelihood of a victim engaging in a physical attack, then, clearly was enhanced by the presence of one or more co-victims.

Table 30. Dispute Outcome (Offender Physical Attack) by Co-offender Presence

Dispute Outcome	Co-offender Presence		
	No	Yes	Total
Non-violent	1184 (67.6%)	650 (54.8%)	1834 (62.4%)
Violent	568 (32.4%)	527 (45.2%)	1105 (37.6%)
Total	1752 (100.0%)	1187 (100.0%)	2939 (100.0%)

χ^2 = 49.568; df = 1; p < .001
Somers' d_{yx} = .128

Table 31. Dispute Outcome (Victim Physical Attack) by Co-victim Presence

Dispute Outcome	Co-victim Presence		Total
	No	Yes	
Non-violent	1385 (80.5%)	703 (73.5%)	2088 (78.0%)
Violent	336 (19.5%)	254 (26.5%)	590 (22.0%)
Total	1721 (100.0%)	957 (100.0%)	2678 (100.0%)

$\chi^2 = 17.633$; df = 1; p < .001
Somers' d_{yx} = .070

Table 32 and Table 33 present data on the distribution of dispute outcome by presence of instigating co-offender(s) and by presence of instigating co-victims(s), respectively. Since co-offenders who were present almost always engaged in instigating behavior, it is not surprising that these data reveal a significant, positive relationship between dispute outcome and the presence of instigating co-offenders (Somers' d_{yx} = .155). Thus, offenders were more likely to engage in a physical attack when they received encouragement or some other form of support from one or more co-offenders than when they were acting alone.[32] The presence of instigating co-victims had a similar effect on victim behavior, significantly increasing the likelihood that the victim would engage in a physical attack (Somers' d_{yx} = .302).

---

[32] The strength of this relationship increases considerably when avoided disputes are excluded from analysis (Somers' d_{yx} = .217).

Table 32. Dispute Outcome (Offender Physical Attack) by Presence of Instigating Co-offender(s)

Dispute Outcome	Instigating Co-offender(s)		Total
	No	Yes	
Non-violent	1184 (67.6%)	530 (52.1%)	1714 (61.9%)
Violent	568 (32.4%)	488 (47.9%)	1056 (38.1%)
Total	1752 (100.0%)	1018 (100.0%)	2770 (100.0%)

$\chi^2 = 65.721$; df = 1; p < .001
Somers' $d_{yx} = .155$

Table 33. Dispute Outcome (Victim Physical Attack) by Presence of Instigating Co-victim(s)

Dispute Outcome	Instigating Co-victim(s)		Total
	No	Yes	
Non-violent	1385 (80.5%)	164 (50.3%)	1549 (75.7%)
Violent	336 (19.5%)	162 (49.7%)	498 (24.3%)
Total	1721 (100.0%)	326 (100.0%)	2047 (100.0%)

$\chi^2 = 135.512$; df = 1; p < .001
Somers' $d_{yx} = .302$

Together, these findings offer support for Hypotheses 7a, 7b, and 7c in showing that the likelihood of dispute-related incidents escalating into violence increased when co-offenders and/or co-victims were present, especially if they instigated.[33] This is consistent with the claim that, in order to maintain an acceptable situated identity, individuals involved in a dispute are likely to conform to the expectations of those around them. However, it is important to note that the strength of the relationships reported above may be artificially inflated by the fact that both co-offenders and co-victims frequently offered encouragement or other forms of support only after the offender and victim, respectively, had engaged in a physical attack.

INTERACTION SEQUENCES
Action Frequencies
Table 34 presents data on the relative frequencies of action type by actor and by type of incident. Similar to Felson's (1984) research, rule-violations, reproaches, orders, non-compliance, and accounts are shown to have occurred frequently, suggesting that the social control process was a crucial factor in these incidents. In addition, the relatively high frequency of identity attacks committed by offenders and victims indicates that altercasting efforts were also important. Although victim accounts and detached worker/third party mediation occurred regularly, they decreased in frequency as incident severity increased. This suggests that accounts and mediation were most likely to occur in response to actions that indicated a high potential for the escalation of disputes.

---

[33] Findings do not differ when the presence of instigating co-offender(s)/instigating co-victim(s) is compared to no co-offender(s)/no co-victim(s) and other types of co-offender(s)/co-victim(s) (i.e., mediating and bystanding) combined (for co-offenders, Somers' $d_{yx} = .157$; for co-victims, Somers' $d_{yx} = .308$).

Table 34. Action Frequencies by Actor and Type of Incident (percentages in parentheses)

Action	All (N = 1238)									
	1	2	3	4	5	6	7	8	9	10
Norm-violation	1 (0.2)	138 (27)	0	0	0	0	0	0	21 (42)	0
Reproach	148 (28.7)	40 (7.8)	0	1 (10)	3 (33.3)	0	0	4 (22.2)	2 (4)	0
Influence Attempt	34 (6.6)	0	0	0	0	0	0	3 (16.7)	0	0
Compliance	2 (0.4)	17 (3.3)	1 (1)	0	0	0	0	0	2 (4)	0
Rebel. Compliance	0	8 (1.6)	0	0	0	0	0	0	2 (4)	0
Non-compliance	8 (1.6)	48 (9.4)	0	0	0	0	0	0	7 (14)	0
Identity Attack	141 (27.3)	55 (10.7)	0	1 (10)	1 (11.1)	0	0	3 (16.7)	5 (10)	0
Non-weapon Threat	31 (6.0)	20 (3.9)	0	0	1 (11.1)	0	0	0	2 (4)	0
Weapon Threat	10 (1.9)	13 (2.5)	0	1 (10)	2 (22.2)	0	0	0	0	0
Evasive Action	5 (1.0)	30 (5.9)	0	1 (10)	0	0	0	0	0	0
Mediation	0	0	99 (95.2)	1 (10)	0	0	0	0	0	0
Instigation	0	0	4 (3.8)	1 (10)	0	1 (100)	0	0	0	0
Account	38 (7.4)	72 (14.1)	0	1 (10)	0	0	0	1 (5.6)	0	0
Physical Attack	69 (13.4)	32 (6.3)	0	3 (30)	1 (11.1)	0	8 (47.1)	3 (16.7)	6 (12)	0
Withdrawal	29 (5.6)	39 (7.6)	0	0	1 (11.1)	0	9 (52.9)	4 (22.2)	3 (6)	1 (100)

1 = Offender Only; 2 = Victim Only; 3 = Third Party; 4 = Co-offender(s) Only; 5 = Co-victim(s) only; 6 = Co-offender(s) and co-victim(s); 7 = Offender and Victim; 8 = Offender and Co-offender(s); 9 = Victim and co-victim (s); 10 = All

Table 34 continued. Action Frequencies by Actor and Type of Incident (percentages in parentheses)

Action					Verbal (N = 711)					
	1	2	3	4	5	6	7	8	9	10
Norm-violation	1 (0.3)	88 (28.7)	0	0	0	0	0	0	13 48.1)	0
Reproach	108 (37.6)	22 (7.2)	0	1 (33.3)	2 (66.7)	0	0	2 (25)	1 (3.7)	0
Influence Attempt	19 (6.6)	0	0	0	0	0	0	1 (12.5)	0	0
Compliance	2 (0.7)	14 (4.6)	1 (1.4)	0	0	0	0	0	2 (7.4)	0
Rebel. Compliance	0	7 (2.3)	0	0	0	0	0	0	2 (7.4)	0
Non-compliance	2 (0.7)	29 (9.4)	0	0	0	0	0	0	3 (11.1)	0
Identity Attack	91 (31.7)	28 (9.1)	0	1 (33.3)	1 (33.3)	0	0	3 (37.5)	2 (7.4)	0
Non-weapon Threat	19 (6.6)	13 (4.2)	0	0	0	0	0	0	2 (7.4)	0
Weapon Threat	0	0	0	0	0	0	0	0	0	0
Evasive Action	4 (1.4)	25 (8.1)	0	0	0	0	0	0	0	0
Mediation	0	0	66 (94.3)	1 (33.3)	0	0	0	0	0	0
Instigation	0	0	3 (4.3)	0	0	0	0	0	0	0
Account	26 (9.1)	59 (19.2)	0	0	0	0	0	1 (12.5)	0	0
Physical Attack	0	0	0	0	0	0	0	0	0	0
Withdrawal	15 (5.2)	22 (7.2)	0	0	0	0	5 (100)	1 (12.5)	2 (7.4)	1 (100)

1 = Offender Only; 2 = Victim Only; 3 = Third Party; 4 = Co-offender(s) Only; 5 = Co-victim(s) only; 6 = Co-offender(s) and co-victim (s); 7 = Offender and Victim; 8 = Offender and Co-offender(s); 9 = Victim and co-victim (s); 10 = All

89

Table 34 continued. Action Frequencies by Actor and Type of Incident (percentages in parentheses)

Action		1	2	3	4	5	6	7	8	9	10
				Verbal With Weapon Threat (N = 57)							
Norm-violation		0	4 (18.2)	0	0	0	0	0	0	2 (100)	0
Reproach		6 (24)	1 (4.5)	0	0	0	0	0	0	0	0
Influence Attempt		1 (4)	0	0	0	0	0	0	0	0	0
Compliance		0	0	0	0	0	0	0	0	0	0
Rebel. Compliance		0	0	0	0	0	0	0	0	0	0
Non-compliance		0	1 (4.5)	0	0	0	0	0	0	0	0
Identity Attack		4 (16)	2 (9.1)	0	0	0	0	0	0	0	0
Non-weapon Threat		1 (4)	0	0	0	0	0	0	0	0	0
Weapon Threat		6 (24)	9 (40.9)	0	0	1 (100)	0	0	0	0	0
Evasive Action		0	1 (4.5)	0	0	0	0	0	0	0	0
Mediation		0	0	5 (100)	0	0	0	0	0	0	0
Instigation		0	0	0	0	0	0	0	0	0	0
Account		3 (12)	2 (9.1)	0	0	0	0	0	0	0	0
Physical Attack		0	0	0	0	0	0	0	0	0	0
Withdrawal		4 (16)	2 (9.1)	0	0	0	0	2 (100)	0	0	0

1 = Offender Only; 2 = Victim Only; 3 = Third Party; 4 = Co-offender(s) Only; 5 = Co-victim(s) only; 6 = Co-offender(s) and co-victim(s); 7 = Offender and Victim; 8 = Offender and Co-offender(s); 9 = Victim and Co-offender(s); 10 = All co-victims

Table 34 continued. Action Frequencies by Actor and Type of Incident (percentages in parentheses)

Action				Physical Attack (N = 360)						
	1	2	3	4	5	6	7	8	9	10
Norm-violation	0	36 (25.5)	0	0	0	0	0	0	2 (18.2)	0
Reproach	28 (17.8)	13 (9.2)	0	0	1 (33.3)	0	0	2 (25)	1 (9.1)	0
Influence Attempt	12 (7.6)	0	0	0	0	0	0	2 (25)	0	0
Compliance	0	2 (1.4)	0	0	0	0	0	0	0	0
Rebel. Compliance	0	1 (0.7)	0	0	0	0	0	0	0	0
Non-compliance	5 (3.2)	13 (9.2)	0	0	0	0	0	0	4 (36.4)	0
Identity Attack	38 (24.2)	18 (12.8)	0	0	0	0	0	0	0	0
Non-weapon Threat	6 (3.8)	7 (5)	0	0	1 (33.3)	0	0	0	0	0
Weapon Threat	1 (0.6)	1 (0.7)	0	0	0	0	0	0	0	0
Evasive Action	1 (0.6)	4 (2.8)	0	0	0	0	0	0	0	0
Mediation	0	0	27 (96.4)	0	0	0	0	0	0	0
Instigation	0	0	1 (3.6)	0	0	1 (100)	0	0	0	0
Account	8 (5.1)	9 (6.4)	0	0	0	0	0	0	0	0
Physical Attack	50 (31.8)	25 (17.7)	0	2 (100)	1 (33.3)	0	7 (77.8)	2 (25)	3 (27.3)	0
Withdrawal	8 (5.1)	12 (8.5)	0	0	0	0	2 (22.2)	2 (25)	1 (9.1)	0

1 = Offender Only; 2 = Victim Only; 3 = Third Party; 4 = Co-offender(s) Only; 5 = Co-victim(s) only; 6 = Co-offender(s) and co-victim(s); 7 = Offender and Victim; 8 = Offender and Co-offender(s); 9 = Victim and co-victims; 10 = All

Table 34 continued. Action Frequencies by Actor and Type of Incident (percentages in parentheses)

					Attempted Weapon Attack (N = 27)					
Action	1	2	3	4	5	6	7	8	9	10
Norm-violation	0	2 (20)	0	0	0	0	0	0	1 (33.3)	0
Reproach	4 (30.8)	2 (20)	0	0	0	0	0	0	0	0
Influence Attempt	0	0	0	0	0	0	0	0	0	0
Compliance	0	0	0	0	0	0	0	0	0	0
Rebel. Compliance	0	0	0	0	0	0	0	0	0	0
Non-compliance	1 (7.7)	0	0	0	0	0	0	0	0	0
Identity Attack	3 (23.1)	1 (10)	0	0	0	0	0	0	2 (66.7)	0
Non-weapon Threat	0	0	0	0	0	0	0	0	0	0
Weapon Threat	1 (7.7)	1 (10)	0	0	0	0	0	0	0	0
Evasive Action	0	0	0	0	0	0	0	0	0	0
Mediation	0	0	1 (100)	0	0	0	0	0	0	0
Instigation	0	0	0	0	0	0	0	0	0	0
Account	0	2 (20)	0	0	0	0	0	0	0	0
Physical Attack	4 (30.8)	2 (20)	0	0	0	0	0	0	0	0
Withdrawal	0	0	0	0	0	0	0	0	0	0

1 = Offender Only; 2 = Victim Only; 3 = Third Party; 4 = Co-offender(s) Only; 5 = Co-victim(s) only; 6 = Co-offender(s) and co-victim(s); 7 = Offender and Victim; 8 = Offender and Co-offender(s); 9 = Victim and co-victims; 10 = All

Table 34 continued. Action Frequencies by Actor and Type of Incident (percentages in parentheses)

Action	Weapon Attack (N = 72)									
	1	2	3	4	5	6	7	8	9	10
Norm-violation	0	7 (24.1)	0	0	0	0	0	0	2 (40)	0
Reproach	1 (3.4)	2 (6.9)	0	0	0	0	0	0	0	0
Influence Attempt	2 (6.9)	0	0	0	0	0	0	0	0	0
Compliance	0	1 (3.4)	0	0	0	0	0	0	0	0
Rebel. Compliance	0	0	0	0	0	0	0	0	0	0
Non-compliance	0	4 (13.8)	0	0	0	0	0	0	0	0
Identity Attack	3 (10.3)	5 (17.2)	0	0	0	0	0	0	1 (20)	0
Non-weapon Threat	5 (17.2)	0	0	0	0	0	0	0	0	0
Weapon Threat	2 (6.9)	2 (6.9)	0	1 (25)	1 (50)	0	0	0	0	0
Evasive Action	0	0	0	1 (25)	0	0	0	0	0	0
Mediation	0	0	0	0	0	0	0	0	0	0
Instigation	0	0	0	0	0	0	0	0	0	0
Account	1 (3.4)	0	0	1 (25)	0	0	0	0	0	0
Physical Attack	13 (44.8)	5 (17.2)	0	1 (25)	0	0	1 (100)	1 (50)	2 (40)	0
Withdrawal	2 (6.9)	3 (10.3)	0	0	1 (50)	0	0	1 (50)	0	0

1 = Offender Only; 2 = Victim Only; 3 = Third Party; 4 = Co-offender(s) Only; 5 = Co-victim(s) only; 6 = Co-offender(s) and co-victim (s); 7 = Offender and Victim; 8 = Offender and Co-offender(s); 9 = Victim and co-victims; 10 = All

93

Event Order

Table 35 presents the mean positions and standard deviations for various unit actions occurring during each type of incident. The order of events generally was similar across all types of incidents. In almost all of the incidents, norm-violations and influence attempts occurred early in interaction sequences, ranking either first or second in overall mean position. The only exception was "attempted weapon attack," in which no orders were issued. Since sufficiently detailed information was provided for only four cases of this type of incident, however, the results may not accurately reflect the typical interaction sequence. Reproaches, identity attacks, and noncompliance usually occurred shortly after norm-violations and influence attempts, with evasive actions following closely behind. In general, accounts were offered in the middle of interaction sequences, after reproaches and threats but before physical attacks. Weapon threats tended to occur after physical attacks without a weapon but before attempted weapon attacks, whereas non-weapon threats tended to occur prior to any type of physical attack. While explicit verbal instigation rarely occurred, its mean position suggests that it sometimes did act as a precursor to physical attacks without a weapon. Finally, mediation, compliance, and submission/withdrawal consistently ended the various types of interaction sequences, occurring after threats as well as physical attacks with or without a weapon.

Similar to Felson's (1984) research on the order of events in four types of incidents (anger, argument, hitting, and weapon), these data show that interaction sequences typically began with norm- and order-violations, after which a social control process was initiated. While identity attacks also occurred fairly early in the interaction sequences, threats and the actual use of violence generally did not occur until later. This is consistent with impression management theory, which claims that the target of an identity attack essentially is compelled to respond aggressively in order to avoid losing face in front of others. Also consistent with impression management theory, actions that minimize or counteract threats to status, such as acquiescence by the offender and/or the victim (i.e., compliance or submission/withdrawal) and mediation efforts on the part of others, typically terminated the incidents.

Table 35. Event Order by Type of Incident

All (N = 1238)				Verbal (N = 711)				Verbal with Weapon Threat (N = 57)			
Action	N	Mean	SD	Action	N	Mean	SD	Action	N	Mean	SD
Influence Attempt	37	0.245	0.080	Influence Attempt	20	0.239	0.090	Norm-violation	6	0.157	0.056
Norm-violation	160	0.268	0.127	Norm-Violation	102	0.278	0.123	Influence Attempt	1	0.330	0.000
Identity Attack	204	0.514	0.237	Non-compliance	34	0.495	0.194	Reproach	7	0.341	0.157
Non-compliance	63	0.515	0.179	Identity Attack	126	0.544	0.235	Non-compliance	1	0.430	0.000
Reproach	198	0.546	0.221	Reproach	136	0.582	0.212	Identity Attack	6	0.452	0.206
Non-weapon Threat	54	0.620	0.191	Non-weapon Threat	34	0.652	0.176	Account/Align. Act.	5	0.500	0.257
Weapon Threat	27	0.620	0.217	Evasive Action	29	0.685	0.218	Evasive Action	1	0.600	0.000
Evasive Action	36	0.665	0.219	Account/Align. Act.	86	0.749	0.222	Weapon Threat	16	0.639	0.191
Account/Align. Act.	112	0.721	0.237	Instigation	3	0.780	0.191	Non-weapon Threat	1	0.800	0.000
Instigation	6	0.723	0.277	Rebel. Compliance	9	0.784	0.239	Mediation	5	0.818	0.052
Rebel. Compliance	121	0.740	0.202	Mediation	67	0.909	0.169	Sub./Withdraw al	8	1.000	0.000
Mediation	10	0.804	0.236	Compliance	19	0.974	0.115	---	---	---	---
Physical Attack	100	0.914	0.158	Sub./Withdraw	46	0.984	0.072	---	---	---	---
Compliance	22	0.952	0.155	---	---	---	---	---	---	---	---
Sub./Withdraw	86	0.983	0.070	---	---	---	---	---	---	---	---

95

Table 35. Event Order by Type of Incident

Physical Attack (N = 360)				Attempted Weapon Attack (N = 27)				Weapon Attack (N = 72)			
Action	N	Mean	SD	Action	N	Mean	SD	Action	N	Mean	SD
Influence Attempt	15	0.241	0.070	Norm-violation	3	0.147	0.040	Influence Attempt	2	0.290	0.057
Norm-violation	38	0.258	0.131	Weapon Threat	2	0.400	0.000	Norm-violation	9	0.301	0.172
Identity Attack	56	0.427	0.217	Reproach	6	0.550	0.280	Reproach	3	0.363	0.162
Reproach	44	0.484	0.222	Account/Align. Act.	2	0.550	0.354	Non-weapon Threat	5	0.488	0.248
Instigation	2	0.500	0.354	Non-compliance	1	0.600	0.000	Account/Align. Act.	2	0.500	0.071
Non-compliance	22	0.538	0.139	Physical Attack	6	0.688	0.242	Identity Attack	9	0.541	0.263
Evasive Action	5	0.568	0.269	Identity Attack	6	0.688	0.295	Non-compliance	4	0.543	0.306
Non-weapon Threat	14	0.577	0.196	Mediation	1	1.000	0.000	Weapon Threat	6	0.545	0.251
Account/Align. Act.	17	0.692	0.267	---	---	---	---	Evasive Action	1	0.640	0.000
Compliance	2	0.725	0.389	---	---	---	---	Physical Attack	23	0.691	0.275
Physical Attack	89	0.750	0.175	---	---	---	---	Sub./Withdraw	7	0.976	0.064
Weapon Threat	3	0.773	0.253	---	---	---	---	Compliance	1	1.000	0.000
Mediation	27	0.939	0.137	---	---	---	---	---	---	---	---
Sub./Withdraw	25	0.978	0.081	---	---	---	---	---	---	---	---
Rebel. Compliance	1	1.000	0.00	---	---	---	---	---	---	---	---

CHAPTER 7

Qualitative Analyses

INTRODUCTION

While quantitative methods permit examination of the general effect of microsocial variables on the occurrence and outcome of dispute-related incidents, they are limited in their ability to reveal the intricacies underlying these social phenomena and to generate novel research questions about them. A qualitative approach is more suited to these tasks. Qualitative research involves interpretations based on observations made of people and events in their natural settings. According to McIntyre (1999:72), the focus is "not only on the objective nature of behavior but on its meaning (or quality)." The first step in qualitative research requires examination of social phenomena as they occur in reality, after which the researcher attempts to uncover patterns in order to build explanations and, ideally, theory. The purpose of adopting this type of inductive approach in the current research was to further understanding of the reasons individuals within the gang context become involved in disputes and why they behave violently in some cases but not in others. Specifically, detached worker and observer reports were combed for themes related to the independent and joint influence of situational factors and interaction processes on both the occurrence and unfolding of disputes. Before turning to the results of these analyses, it is necessary to discuss the background contexts that structured interaction processes among gang boys and between gang boys and others.

CONTEXTUAL THEMES

Although this study focuses primarily on the importance of features operating in the foreground of dispute-related incidents (i.e., microsocial factors and processes and their interactions), background conditions were important. Four themes emerged from the observational data.

First, race, class, and gang membership clearly were major background factors in the lives of the gang boys, and each was important as these boys negotiated their way through adolescence. Gang boys identified themselves and were identified by others according to the gang to which they belonged. Gangs were always racially homogeneous, and membership typically coincided with residence in a particular geographic area (within lower-class neighborhoods of Chicago). Relationships between gangs were rooted in tradition, with inter-gang rivalries and friendships generally persisting over time. Nevertheless, "peace treaties" and "truces," almost always facilitated by the detached workers, occasionally alleviated or eliminated hostilities between rival gangs. Temporary alliances also were formed between rival gangs when conflict developed with a group of individuals of a different race, suggesting that racial identity underlay gang identity.[34] In a social environment divided largely on the basis of race (see Short and Strodtbeck 1965), gang identification was the most immediate concern for gang boys, and inter-gang rivalries and violence were always intra-racial (see Appendix B for racial classification of gangs).[35] In those rare cases involving confrontation with members of another race, however, racial identification invariably took precedence over allegiance to any one gang. Even a lengthy history of inter-gang antagonism did not prevail over the importance of race, as indicated in the following report of three rival black gangs—the Cobras/Warriors, the Imperials, and the Vice Lords:

---

[34] The fact that members of one's own race were often excluded as acceptable targets of predatory violence also highlights the importance of racial identity.

[35] Similarly, Gary Schwartz (1987:107) reports that racial conflict occurred largely at the periphery of the social world of youth residing in a working-class community undergoing racial transition.

Thursday night is when I saw all those Cobras and many Imperials, about 45 to 50 kids, and Vice Lords, too. They never, never stand out there and drink wine together. They were on 16th Street drinking wine together, talking and laughing. This was all because of the incident of the boy who supposedly was an Imperial and was shot and killed. They claim that some white boys shot him, and it was all directed around that. It was Imperials mostly...Warriors were mostly buying drinks for the Vice Lords because they wanted to get their help to go over there and jack up some guys. This was over around Harrison High, in that neighborhood. (Detached Worker Report, Gilmore, July 17, 1961)

Second, observations by detached workers and others suggest that, even though gang boys faced constant pressure to maintain status, often through the use of violence, their concerns and behaviors, for the most part, were normal and rational. Facilitated by the direction and opportunities provided by detached workers, most of the gangs were organized and operated much like conventional social clubs, with a recognized leadership structure, scheduled meetings and elections, business-like negotiations with other gangs, membership dues, and pre-planned events. Aside from a heavy emphasis on getting high and the acceptance of violence to settle disputes or to strong-arm others, the daily activities of individual members were also largely conventional. Much of their time was spent taking steps to obtain a job, participating in sports, making plans and preparations for the future (e.g., enlisting in the Navy), and socializing with male and female peers. With few exceptions, gang boys were often reluctant to engage in violence (though they did attempt to conceal their hesitance), and in cases in which violence appeared to be imminent, they were generally realistic about not acting foolishly if faced with overwhelming odds or if there was a high likelihood of getting into trouble with the law, the YMCA, their detached worker, and/or fellow gang members. Most of the gang boys also showed respect for persons in positions of authority, such as their detached worker and police officers. Similar to findings from Elijah Anderson's (1999) poignant study of social types residing in poor-inner city neighborhoods, individual gang members and gangs as groups tended to exhibit "decent" values despite strong and pervasive social pressures to adopt "street" values and behave unconventionally.

Another emergent theme involves the normative structure and sanctioning system that operated within the social milieu of the gang boys. Countervailing conventional and unconventional pressures constrained gang members' behavior and their status within the gang; excess in either direction could result in ridicule, relegation to the fringe, or even ostracism, as happened in several cases in which a gang boy became heavily involved in school or family matters or, conversely, beat his mother, did too many drugs, or caused too much trouble with fellow gang members, rival gangs, or the law. As long as they were not too self-centered or "square," status generally was conferred upon those gang members who possessed some sort of special ability or skill (such as with the girls or in athletics, street smarts, or singing and dancing) or who had access—authorized or unauthorized—to alcohol, cars, money, "sharp" clothes, or other desirable commodities.[36] While leadership positions typically were reserved for those adept at fighting, the majority of gang boys settled on alternative means of achieving status, even if relatively short-lived. Those who were in some way socially deficient (e.g., illiterate, physically deformed, from a bad home environment, etc.) were the most likely to behave violently (if capable), largely because their opportunities to achieve status in other ways were limited. Furthermore, those who had established reputations as fighters were not required to demonstrate their toughness repeatedly, and they were unlikely targets of challenges and harassment by others. Provided that they exercised discretion, then, gang members who had proven themselves as proficient fighters were rewarded with status and thus influence within the gang. Gang members could also achieve status, albeit not to the same extent or as lasting in effect, by excelling in more conventional activities or through the legitimate or illegitimate obtainment of symbols of adulthood. There were definite limits on delinquent and violent behaviors and the more conventional means of achieving status, however, and gang members who did not operate within these confines were likely to suffer a loss of status.

---

[36] A detached worker indicated that "the girls judge the guys as the guys are judged by the other guys" (Detached Worker Report, Oldham, February 27, 1962).

Finally, the data clearly demonstrate the important role that detached workers played in the social milieu of the gang boys. While worker effectiveness depended on such factors as how strongly they opposed delinquent behaviors and their rapport with gang boys, all of the workers succeeded in pushing gangs and individual members away from delinquent activities in most cases. As noted by Short et al. (1964:64), the detached worker role "may be seen as compensatory for 'deficits' in gang boys' relations with other adult roles." Workers were the strongest—and, frequently, the only—link that these boys had to conventional society. They did special favors for them, supporting them in court and in other contacts with the law, getting them out of trouble with their parents, helping them locate employment, giving them use of rooms in which to hold their club meetings, and taking them for car rides. They also provided the boys with opportunities to participate in sports, YMCA dances and events, and a variety of other legitimate activities. Thus, the workers had a great deal of leverage over the boys and, perhaps more important, a means by which to forge close relationships with those in leadership positions. By threatening a loss of privileges and having core members play an active role in the control of other gang members and in negotiations for peace with rival gangs, workers usually were able to manipulate the behavior of the boys in the desired direction. Furthermore, as noted by the workers, gang boys were often reluctant to enter into violent situations and therefore welcomed intervention efforts.[37]

Summary

Together, these themes provide an important context within which disputes occurred and unfolded. On one hand, inter-racial hostilities, inter-gang rivalries, and status concerns all contributed to violence. The importance of status was also associated with other types of delinquent behaviors. On the other hand, however, pressures from detached workers and other gang members to act in accordance with conventional behavioral standards, as well as internalized standards of decency and a propensity for rationality, worked in the opposite

---

[37] When all else failed, workers could themselves intervene physically and/or solicit intervention from the police.

direction. In order to maintain acceptable social- and self-identities, then, gang members were required to balance expectations for delinquency and violence against the demands for more conventional behaviors, conforming to a certain extent to both but exceeding the limits of neither.

NARRATIVE DATA
Setting
Qualitative analysis of the data provides a great deal of insight into the influence of the setting in dispute-related incidents. Consistent with quantitative findings, public places (e.g., streets, street corners, parks, and local gymnasiums), particularly where both the offender and victim typically hung out, were mentioned frequently as settings in which disputes were likely to emerge. This is to be expected, as the majority of reports are based on incidents observed directly by the detached worker and/or observer, both of whom spent most of their time in the field attending various activities, such as dances and sporting events, or just hanging on the street corner or in a poolroom with gang members.

Quantitative data revealed that approximately one in four (25.6%) dispute-related incidents emerged in the territory of one party but not the other. However, qualitative analysis of the data indicates that disputes involving explicit territorial (or "turf") concerns actually were much less frequent, occurring only when the offender and victim were members of a different race or rival gangs. In order to understand territorial disputes, then, it is necessary that they be contextualized in terms of black-white relationships as well as inter-gang relationships.

The Inter-racial Context
Short and Strodtbeck (1965:112) note that, during the period of observation (1959-1962), nearly all lower-class white neighborhoods in Chicago were undergoing racial transition and that white opposition to black invasion involved both adults and adolescents. The "rowdyism" of white young people that their elders frequently complained about thus could be "turned to advantage" when it involved aggression directed at blacks. Although this widespread hostility meant that threats

of violence against blacks and action toward that end became commonplace, white on black attacks—whether undertaken specifically in "defense" of turf or were more opportunistic in nature—did not progress beyond physical pursuits and property destruction in these data, except in the rare cases when black victims were resistant (see Anderson, June 14, 1962, in "victim resistance").

The following case, excerpted from a detached worker report, shows the reaction of members of a white gang (the Dukes) and other white boys to information that some "colored kids" were in "their" park:

> The following Friday night, after the dance at St. Francis, Tom and myself and a couple of guys did go over to Rossi's [restaurant]…a goodly crowd there, I'd say about 20 or 30 kids. Freddie comes barreling in from across the street, and he started going from table to table whispering, and pretty soon the guys started to get up and leave. I was sitting with some guys and Tom at the front table, and I noticed all the Dukes…they were primarily Dukes, although actually it was most of the guys in the place…they started to drift out. So, I followed them out. I noticed they all clustered in the corner going across the street into Rich's car. He had a flat tire at the time, and he was fixing it across the street in this gas station. They all clustered around his car, and it looked like there were weapons being passed out in the form of clubs and jack handles, etc. All of a sudden, they barrel-assed down Dobson, heading towards 78th and the park. I knew something was up, so I drifted out behind them, and when I saw them walking down towards 78th Street, I followed them. They got three-quarters of the way down the street, and they stopped and started to talk back and forth very heatedly and then they turned around and came back. I said, "What's up fellows?" They said, "We heard there were some coloreds down there in the park. We're not ready to give in that easily to them. We were going to go down there and throw them out." Then, they all backtracked to Rossi's. Apparently, they encountered somebody coming up from the park who said that there were no colored kids down there and that disbanded the group. (Detached Worker Report, Lamotte, April 12, 1960)

Despite their relative infrequency, interracial conflicts also emerged in predominantly black neighborhoods. An observer reported the following incident in which a white man was badly beaten by some blacks (including members of the Nobles) in black territory:

> As I was talking to some of the Nobles, a white man [age about 28, red hair, nicely dressed] approached the corner. He leaned over on the lamppost, as if he were drunk or having a regurgitation, and he wretched several times. One of the Nobles' baseball players [short center on the team] said, "That sloppy white mother-fucker should be ashamed of himself for dirtying up our neighborhood." One of the other fellows said, "Well, what does he think he's doing over in our neighborhood anyway?" While the fellow was still hanging on to the lamppost, several men came out of the tavern and walked over to him and asked him how was he. The fellow mumbled something inaudible to my ears. The short center of the Nobles went over to the several men who had collected around the fellow, and two other young men [non-Nobles, non-Players] followed. The latter two young men hit the man. After he fell, most of the men standing around kicked him. Several of those adults standing around made rather vituperative statements about the unnecessary nature of the white man's trip into the area. One exclaimed, "Well, it serves his ass right. He has no business in this neighborhood anyway, and if they caught you alone in one of their neighborhoods or walking on one of their beaches they would surely kick your ass." One of the young men ripped his pockets open and said, "He might as well supply our wine money." The Nobles' short center then said, "Yeah man, we'll get a good high on tonight." The three young men who had done most of the beating of the fellow walked back over to where we were standing and began to pull the dollar bills out of his wallet. The Nobles' short center, upon seeing me gaze at him in a questioning manner, told me that he had been chased off of the beaches too often at 71st, 75th, and 79th this summer to really care whether or not they killed the mother fucker. Just about this time, Bobby and the rest of the Nobles came out of the Pig and Whistle [a local pool hall] and walked up and started

asking questions. Most of the fellows who had participated in the foray were slowly drifting down 3rd Street, leaving only me looking at the unconscious figure on the sidewalk. Bobby and Sidney asked me if I had seen the whole thing. I quietly told them yes. Blood was trickling down the left side of his face. I told Bobby that I thought that someone ought to call the police to get him to the hospital before he bleeds to death. He laughed and said that the mother fucker ought to bleed in the gutter so that it would not leave a spot on their favorite corner. (Observer Report, Wright, August 8, 1960)

Serious violence such as this was rare, but inter-racial disputes over territory could be dangerous for both whites and blacks. Territorial infringements, whether intentional or not, always were accompanied by the potential for some sort of violent conflict.

The Inter-gang Context
In contrast to inter-racial neighborhood disputes, *gang* territorial disputes in these data were always intra-racial and black.[38] Workers' frequent references to "peace" arrangement efforts between gangs and to obtaining "permission" to enter each other's territory reflect the nature of inter-gang relationships and the role of detached workers. Because detached workers actively sought to avoid territorial confrontation, overt disputes between gangs over territory were rare. In these data, only when offender and victim were members of rival gangs did such disputes emerge. The importance of territorial concerns in these cases is readily apparent in both detached worker and observer reports. In the following excerpt, for example, the detached worker for the Junior Imperials describes an incident that took place in response to the Vice Lords locating their clubroom in Imperial territory:

This all started Friday afternoon, when Jerry took it upon himself to go over to the Vice Lords' clubhouse...in the heart of our [Imperials'] area. They had a big sign painted "Vice

---

[38] Violent confrontations between white and black gangs did not occur in these data. Both black and white gang boys were reluctant to enter into territory occupied predominantly by members of a different race, often expressing concern for their safety.

Lords' Dance to be Held Here Tonight," and Jerry went over and tore the sign down and walked into the basement where they held the dance last week and tore the sign up and threw it on the table. So, Ernest, the vice-president of the Vice Lords, told him not to let it happen again. Jerry said, "I'll do it again if you put the sign up, and nobody's going to do anything about it." So, Ernest invited him outside, and he wouldn't go and then Ernest claims he hurt his hand during the fight, so he picked up a stick and of course Jerry wouldn't fight him anymore, and when Ernest picked up the stick, he took off. After Jerry left, he returned with some of the Midgets [Midget Imperials] and kicked down the door of the clubhouse, but the Vice Lords had by that time already left. That evening, as soon as I got in touch with Larry [president of the Junior Imperials], we went over to the Vice Lords' clubhouse and talked to Ernest and their president, and we told them that we didn't feel that Jerry was justified in what he had done, but we didn't feel either that their clubroom should be in that area, but actually being as we were on peace, it didn't make that much difference. So, the thing was ironed out then and there, and Ernest even invited the guys back there and then to the dance. So, we returned to the 16th Street area, and on the way back, Larry told Jerry that he was wrong in tearing the sign down, and Jerry complained that they were in our territory and they should be on the other side of Central Park. I explained that we were on peace terms with the Vice Lords and actually they could have dances in our area if they wanted to because we weren't fighting with them. Then, I asked him what he would have done if the Juniors were having a dance and Ernest came over and tore the sign off the wall there. He said, "We'd have gone (inaudible)." I said, "That's just what happened in his case." He felt that he was backed up against a wall and had to defend himself...what you or me or anyone else would have done. (Detached Worker Report, Mitchell, September 29, 1959)

Reporting on what he had been told about the same incident, the field observer who often accompanied this worker states:

> Ed Mitchell told me that Jerry had proceeded to excite many of the members of his gang by shading the story enough so that it would seem that Ernest's threat was the most important item in the story. Many of them easily forgot that Jerry was the actual instigator. Mitchell said that to many of the Imperials the immediate question was the one concerning the territorial infringement of Ernest's boys. (Observer Report, Wright, September 25, 1959)

Two years later, the detached worker for the Vice Lords reported an incident in which members of the Cobras were physically attacked by the Vice Lords in Cobra territory. Upon questioning the leader of the Vice Lords (Pep), the worker discovers that at least part of the reason for the attack was that the Vice Lords were upset about previous territorial infringements committed by the Cobras:

> The group's [Vice Lords] activity on Labor Day consisted of, for the most part, going to the show and wolf-packing later that night. They went over to K-Town, beating up members of the Cobras. This happened at approximately 10:30 Monday night. I asked Pep about it Tuesday, why they went over to Cobra territory wolf-packing. He told me that the group and he were tired of the police pushing them around and the Cobras trying to move into their territory. (Detached Worker Report, Gilmore, September 9, 1961)

When a member or members of one race or gang encroached upon the turf of another, violence was likely. However, four situational factors were associated with non-violent resolutions of territorial disputes: (1) unequal armament; (2) imbalanced numbers; (3) fearsome reputation; and (4) mediation.

First, violence in disputes involving territorial concerns was likely to be squashed when an unarmed party offered little or no resistance to the opposing party due to latter's possession of weaponry, whether real or perceived. An example of this process was reported by the detached worker for the Midget Imperial Chaplains:

[About two or three weeks ago], one of the Vice Lords came around and fired a gun in the air twice and said, "Give me this corner," and most of the guys [Midget Imperial Chaplains] didn't have any weapons, none of the guys, and they were afraid and moved off the corner. The Vice Lord that had been firing the gun had been drinking and they figured they might get hit by a stray bullet, so they left. So, they wanted to make sure this didn't happen anymore, so they brought their weapons out and were imitating...firing in the air and saying, "give me this corner" bit. But, they fired and ran. I picked them up and took them home and told them to put the guns away, give them back to their parents, or if they were theirs just put them up. (Detached Worker Report, Brown, February 23, 1961)

Later that same year, the worker with the Vice Lords reported another incident involving the Vice Lords, although this time their adversaries were members of the Cobras:

About 5 or 6 incidents have happened where the Vice Lords were on the worst end. They have had 4 or 5 guys get shot, and one Lord got beat up. These things were done by the Midget Cobras, and it was said that the Comanche, who are supposed to be broken up, jumped on one of the Vice Lords and beat him up. George and I were pretty successful in stopping retaliation. I guess in order to prove to the kids in the neighborhood, they made this walk down 16th. They also did the same thing through K-Town. They lined up one night about 30 strong and walked west on 16th. I called the police that night. They [the Vice Lords] came back on 14th Street looking for Cobras. They stopped in the Cobras' favorite hangout, a tavern on 14th and Carlo, and went in there. As they got ready to walk out, Calloway wrote "Vice Lords" on the wall, and they walked back with no trouble, just to prove that they are still strong. I guess the Cobras imagined they had weapons on them. Pep is on the picture definitely, but he led the groups through Imperial and Cobra territory. I'd say he had about 20 each time. (Detached Worker Report, Gilmore, December 21, 1961)

In these incidents, the Vice Lords openly infringed upon rival gang territories (Midget Imperial Chaplains' and Cobras', respectively). However, in both cases, the Vice Lords' superior armament—real or perceived—appeared to have prevented their rivals from fighting back. While it is possible that the Cobras were outnumbered by the Vice Lords and did not respond with violence for that reason, evidence from the previous incident between a lone armed Vice Lord and several unarmed Imperials lends credibility to the worker's statement that "the Cobras imagined they [the Vice Lords] had weapons on them." Gang territorial disputes such as these, then, were likely to be resolved non-violently when only one party was armed or at least was believed by the other (unarmed) party to be armed.

Other cases support the role of unbalanced numbers in non-violent resolutions of territorial disputes. The following incident in which 50 to 60 of the Cobras walked through Vice Lord territory without encountering resistance is apposite:

> For the last six months the Vice Lords have been the biggest and most powerful group on the West Side. Sometimes it's the Cobras and sometimes it's the Vice Lords, and this has been going on continually. Now, recently, within the past 2 months, the Cobras have started to get pretty strong in numbers, and one day they got permission from the leadership structure of the Vice Lords to walk through Vice Lord City. This was when they were going to jump on the Braves. Well, since that time, they have been feeling free to walk through. They came through a week ago Wednesday and some of them were looking for trouble and they kind of caught the Lords by surprise. There must have been about 50 to 60 of them, too many of them for the Vice Lords to handle. They didn't push their weight around too much, but they were there in force and frightened the Vice Lords to the point where they thought the Cobras were going to jump on them. I was at the Y when it happened and George was up there and he told me about it, that the Cobras had the Vice Lords up tight, outnumbered by about 3 to 1, but nothing came of it. But, afterwards, every time I would talk to some of the fellows about the situation, they kept talking about getting themselves together before the Cobras came through and started something. I heard them

talking that "we're not going to let Cobras come through here anymore." Last night, they planned on if the Cobras had come through...and I told the police officers that really work close with them. I told them about it, what they had planned if the Cobras came through there, and they said they would keep an eye on them and told me to keep them away from Holland and they would keep the Cobras out of the territory, and they didn't come through, although there were quite a few guys waiting on the corner for them to come through. (Detached Worker Report, Gilmore, November 9, 1961)

Although the Cobras committed a serious territorial infringement against the Vice Lords and thereby openly challenged their status, the fact that the Vice Lords were badly outnumbered appeared to be the main reason for a non-violent resolution of the dispute. Not until outnumbered disputants were capable of "getting themselves together" would they be expected (by themselves and others) to do battle.

Territorial dispute outcomes also were affected by especially fearsome reputations on the street, as in the following case:

Pep is more aggressive. He went over to the Midget Imperial area and made them get off the corner, either Sunday or Monday. He went over there and told them to get off the corner. There was a group of them. Larry Walker, a Senior...heard about it from the Imperials. He said, "I want this corner," trying to pick a fight. Jimmy Gunn was out there, Harry, Harvey, a couple of the Juniors, about 7 Vice Lords and about 15 Imperials, and they walked to the Imperials' territory and the Imperials, not wanting a fight...and guys like Larry are not prone to this kind of fighting. They have really grown out of this and they are guys over in Imperial territory and he just happened to come up at a right time and these guys did move off and they brought it back to me. Willie brought it to me and Willie is a pretty nice guy that lived through all of this Filmore trouble. He and Pep were good friends, so he didn't think that Pep was speaking to him, because he was sitting in his car and he brought it to me that the rest of the guys moved off. (Detached Worker Report, Gilmore, August 4, 1961)

While Pep of the Vice Lords clearly was "trying to pick a fight" with the Imperials in their own territory, the Imperials apparently did not feel so compelled by status concerns to resist him and simply complied with his order to give him their corner, even though they outnumbered the Vice Lords about 15 to 7. The worker for the Vice Lords, not having been present at the time of the incident, attributed the Imperials' lack of resistance to their maturation out of fighting. However, the worker for the Imperials continued to report fighting incidents involving the Imperials—at times against the Vice Lords—for approximately six months following this report. Since Pep was recognized by both the Vice Lords and the Imperials as one of the toughest amongst all gang leaders, as indicated on numerous occasions by several of the workers, it is reasonable to conclude that the Imperials backed down from violence because of their opponent's fearsome reputation. Indeed, individuals who made the anomalous and unwise decision to challenge a fearsome opponent not only were likely to be badly beaten but were likely to be ridiculed by their peers as well:

Yancey...had an argument and ultimately a fight with a boy that used to be in the Senior Imperials and who they all call Blinky. This boy works regular, but he drinks rather heavily. Weeks ago, Blinky had a fight with Pep, and he was beat up pretty bad, and Yancey was teasing him about it, and the two of them had a fight there. Before too many blows had passed, I had managed to separate them and the police came. Yancey fled while the other boy stood up and talked to the police and told them what had happened. (Detached Worker Report, Walker, May 7, 1962)

Finally, mediation by detached workers and/or other third parties often prevented the escalation of territorial disputes into violence. Excerpted from a report made by the detached worker with the Midget Imperial Chaplains, the following incident provides an example of the pivotal role of mediation:

After the game, my boys dressed and we went over to the Elks Hall, where they have their regular dance every Friday night. This night, the Vice Lords were to come to the Elks Hall for the first time. They had made a peace treaty with the

Imperials. There was one small incident where Lester [he's in the Imperials] resented the fact that the Vice Lords were able to come to the Elks Hall, which was previously dominated by Imperials and a few of the Cobras and the Braves. This incident was expected by myself and the other workers from the CYC, so it was stopped before it began. This is the only incident that happened inside the hall itself. Lester always drinks a little. I think this might have been the reason for him wanting to start something, but not the main reason. Lester just likes to agitate. They call him Little Lying Lester and he tells lies on top of lies all the time. This is his favorite pastime. (Detached Worker Report, Brown, January 20, 1961)

Although the details of this incident are sketchy, mediation efforts of the detached worker and/or CYC workers appear to have prevented Lester (and perhaps some of the other Imperials) from responding with violence to the status threat represented by the Vice Lords' entry into Imperial territory. Thus, in addition to reducing the frequency with which gang territorial disputes emerged, worker intervention often was an important factor in the non-violent resolution of such confrontations.

In sum, qualitative analysis reveals the importance of location in dispute-related incidents. By their very nature, such incidents occurred most often in public places, usually where both the offender and victim (and detached workers/observers) hung out. Disputes with a territorial component were relatively rare, however, occurring only when the offender and victim were members of different races or rival gangs. Although group norms favoring defense of turf meant that violence was common in these cases, the relationship between territory and dispute outcome clearly was not a perfect one. These data show that non-violent outcomes could be expected mainly when the operation of other situational factors suggested to gang boys that backing down from violence was less costly than acting violently. That is, either the odds of both physical harm and social humiliation were high (fearsome reputation of opponent) or a face-saving reason for retreat was coupled with the possibility that violence would lead to serious physical harm (numerical or weapons disadvantage) or social disapproval (detached worker/third party mediation). Even when status concerns were heightened by the fact that rights to turf were at stake, then, the impact of weapons, the relative number of co-offenders and co-victims, opponent reputation, and audience behavior on the impression management process was vital to the decision made by gang boys to engage in or retreat from violence.

Offender-victim Relationship

Quantitative findings revealed that disputes were most likely to involve a gang member against an individual with no known gang affiliation (e.g., detached worker), followed in order by disputes between members of different gangs, members of the same gang, and non-gang individuals. However, violent outcomes were shown to be more characteristic of disputes involving members of rival gangs than disputes involving any other type of offender-victim gang relationship. Qualitative analysis sheds light on the reasons behind these general patterns and the circumstances that tended to produce divergences. Intra-gang, inter-gang (both rival and friendly), extra-group, and non-group dispute-related incidents are discussed in turn.

Intra-gang disputes often occurred as a result of norm-violations (39.4%) and identity attacks (25.2%)[39] or retaliation for such things as rat-finking (17.7%). Frequently, disputants in such cases were intoxicated (one party only = 53.2%; both parties = 44.6%). Unless the gang lacked any real cohesion, however, these types of disputes were likely to be resolved without violence (64.0%). The data suggest three explanations for this finding: (1) the detached worker and/or other third parties mediated; (2) one of the parties of the dispute backed down in order to avoid embarrassment linked to violence with a gang member who was severely intoxicated,[40] physically disabled, small in stature, or otherwise socially inadequate; and (3) one of the parties of the dispute

---

[39] "Signifying" (putting another down) was a prominent feature of interaction between gang members. On occasion, gang boys were observed "playing the dozens," an impromptu competition involving a rapid exchange of insults (see Berdie 1947).

[40] In several cases, one gang member was intoxicated to such an extent that fellow gang members saw an opportunity to "get their cracks in" without any chance of serious repercussions. However, this appeared to occur only during periods of instability in the gang's cohesiveness.

submitted to the other due to the latter's high ranking position within the gang and/or apparent willingness to engage in violence. An observer's report shows the significance of some of these factors and processes, alone and in combination:

> After the basketball game was over, Al [detached worker— Stateway Cobras], Benny Ross, and I went into Mr. Ford's office and stood around the desk talking. Mr. Ford went out into the lobby. Just as Mr. Ford returned, Benny told us that he thinks that a fight is coming up outside. We all look out of the picture window and see Larry taking off his coat and Rat standing opposite him, telling him that he will kick his ass. Rat is about 4'10" while Larry is about 5'8" tall. Both of the boys are seemingly intoxicated and talking rather incoherently and vociferously. Rat implies in his diatribes at Larry that Larry should not consider his size but just try and kick his ass. Larry in his retort to these statements implies that since Rat is such a small person it would be embarrassing to kick his ass and really below his dignity. Larry's statements seem to only intensify the brandishing by Rat. None of the spectators seem to be terribly impressed by the threats of Rat. Several of them laugh when Al tells Larry to put his coat back on and tells Rat to go home. Rat then turns on the crowd and tells them that he will kick anybody's ass who dares step off of the curb. His threat only serves to draw more laughter. Just about this time, Bernard comes out of the field house and asks who it is that is fighting. Being in a rather peripheral position, I tell him that it is a drunken Rat trying to get anyone to fight him. Bernard yelled to him that, if he doesn't quit all that noise and profanity, he will really kick his ass and send him home. Rat glared at Bernard for a moment and decides in his partial stupor that here is someone who is his own size and who really means what he says. Rat trundled on off toward the street mumbling something about "getting his brother to come back and kick everybody's ass for picking on him." Bernard heard all this and ran down the street after him and put his arm around his shoulder in a rather brotherly manner as if to comfort him. (Observer Report, Wright, December 18, 1959)

These incidents demonstrate how potential violence among members of the same gang (in this case, the Stateway Cobras) generally was squashed, even when at least one of the participants was intoxicated. In the first incident, Larry backed down from Rat because of the potential loss of face he would suffer if he were to beat up someone who clearly was so much smaller. As the observer reported, "Larry in his retort to these statements [made by Rat] implies that since Rat is such a small person it would be embarrassing to kick his ass and really below his dignity." Mediation by the detached worker further ensured a non-violent outcome. In the second incident, Rat backed down from his new opponent, Bernard, who appeared ready to engage in violence. Since Rat indicated a willingness to do battle with a much larger opponent in the previous incident with Larry, fear of physical injury does not offer a complete explanation for his withdrawal from an opponent of approximately equal size in this incident. Thus, it seems reasonable to conclude that Rat backed down to avoid the greater loss of status that would result from being beaten by an individual who was described as being "his [Rat's] own size" and as someone who "really means what he says" than by an individual who had an obvious physical advantage but who appeared to be more reluctant to engage in violence. In cases involving intra-gang members, then, violence was most likely to be squashed when a member or members of the external audience intervened; when the poor situational identity of one party served as an indication to the opposing party that violence was not needed to maintain status and that, if undertaken, potentially would result in a loss of face; or when one party perceived backing down (a behavior often accompanied by some assurance of retaliation) to be less costly than fighting a person who was likely to win or otherwise inflict unwanted physical and social harm.

The majority of inter-gang disputes involved members of two rival gangs (at least 72.6%), not members of two friendly gangs. While the latter sometimes had fights, such as when there were problems between divisions of the same gang nation (i.e., Seniors, Juniors, Midgets) and/or when intoxicants were involved, non-violent outcomes were more typical (60.3%). The main reason for this finding is that detached workers and third parties frequently mediated in these disputes.

Unlike disputes involving members of friendly gangs, disputes involving members of rival gangs were characterized by a great deal of violence (59.3%), including some of the most vicious fights, beatings, and gun battles reported. Although retaliation motives were evident in many of these disputes (57.0%), the high rate of violence also appeared to be a function of the heightened status concerns—gang and individual—frequently present in this context. An apposite case is the following lengthy excerpt from an interview with the Vice Lords' detached worker:

On the 24th, Friday, they had a big dance at Elks Hall. I walked in there and saw C. Archer, Junior, Possum, Polecat, Billy…about 6. Archer was talking to one of the Cobras that he knew in there. When I walked in, he called me over to the side and said, "Later on, this stuff is going to happen when more of the fellows come in." Tojo [Vice Lord] was with me. A lot of the Midget and Junior Imperials were up there. Some of the Cobras and a few of the Lords were there. About half an hour went by and Stumpdaddy [leader of the K-Town Cobras] walked in, and he was talking with Tojo over in the corner because they were in jail together and they had most of the stuff ironed. While he was doing it, Polecat took out his knife, opened it up, and looked at me. I shook my head, but he kept it open. But, he didn't do anything. Some of the other Cobras that came over to talk were talking to Tojo and Stumpdaddy. Everything was sort of mellow at this time. Tommy was recognized right away when he came in. Stump started talking to him and told him what they had been talking about and said, "Hell, we might as well have peace." But, Tommy didn't want to listen to them. So, Stump said, "Well, I am not going to kiss your ass over it. If you guys want to fight, we'll fight." At this time, the Cobras were loaded in there; there were 60 Cobras at least. They came over there strictly to fight because they heard this stuff was going to go down that night. So, they were prepared. Before, when Stump was talking to Tojo, I didn't like what was going on, so I told Jenkins [detached worker for the Cobras] to tell Veronica [adult] to go out and call the police because things weren't right. They got there late. Tojo was trying to talk to Stump. He asked him what was wrong, and one of the Cobras came up and tried to get in it. He said, "We would just as soon fight you." Tojo jumped back. With a couple of "yo ho's" in there, chairs started flying...I got them [Vice Lords] all out except for Junior and Tojo. Junior was in the middle of the floor with about 60 Cobras around him, and he was going to fight. I grabbed his arm and said, "You dumb shit, get yourself outside. You got no chance out here." I told Tojo not to move...just watch the chairs. A couple policemen were in there. They got their guns out and broke (inaudible). It got to where I said, "Tojo, it's about time for us to leave now." We saw the Cobras and the Imperials break for the other door. So, we went down the other stairs. The big fight broke out outside. It was out of hand. Tommy had run across the street and got the sawed-off shotgun. The police shot two times up in the air and...I was breaking up individual fights. The Cobras...boy, when they got doubled up together, they have a line of about 10, 8 or 9 deep, and they just march like this. I stopped them a couple of times, but 8 or 9 were on Calloway, and Calloway was sharp that day. He had his cape on and a green coat, a brand new hat, and a new umbrella, like Zorro. He was beating guys on the side of the head with that umbrella. When he was through, the metal was bent all over. It just looked like a piece of string. They had gotten him up against a car and were getting to him. So, I jumped between the Cobras and Calloway and swung him around. I told him to get his ass out. He said, "Man, where's my hat?" I said, "You're lucky you got your ass. Forget your hat." So, I got the guys off Calloway, and over on this Ogden side, about 3 of them had C. Archer over there, and Archer had a big stick in his left hand and was about ready to use this stick when Hank took the stick away from him. I jumped between the Cobras and C. Archer, and got all of the Cobras off except for Flukey. Flukey and C. Archer had each other. They were clean, so I said, "You guys stay out of it. These two guys wanted each other for a long time, you dig." I always did go for a good humbug, so I let them go and let them fight. They humbugged each other until they got tired or got hurt and then they quit. About 4 Lords were fighting and maybe 60 Cobras, but all of them didn't throw a punch. The rest of the Lords sold out because they didn't have no strength. The wheels in the Lords weren't there, and they expected Tommy to do something. He broke across the street to get his shotgun, but he never came back. The ones that stood their ground were Tojo, Henry, C. Archer, Vernon, and Calloway, and all of them had marks of battle on them. They got whipped but not beat badly, and the Cobras respect them for staying. They have no respect for Tommy because he sold out. They don't respect none of the other fellows that sold out. A lot of respect for Calloway because he stood his ground. Those guys gained a lot of prestige in one night. It was all fist fighting, except for Calloway, who was using his umbrella. After I broke the last fight up between C. Archer and about 8 or 9 of the Cobras, I was watching and just moving back and forth. One of the boys [Tommy Lee] had a shotgun, but he didn't use it, because the time he was going to use it, the two detectives had their backs to him, and there was Calloway and a couple other Lords up against the wall, so he didn't pull the trigger. He was across the street. When there were so many Cobras, he didn't break across Ogden. He stood over there and watched. With Jenkins, I finally got the Cobras to stop. I swung the Cobras around and told them to stop...Flukey, Stump, Gray Ghost, Count Dracula, Jonell...some of the wheels in the Cobras that I know real well...turned them around and told them to stop the shit because "the man is going to be here in a couple of minutes and he is going to bust us all." The Lords kept going down 16th Street until they got toward home. Calloway was mad as can be, his hair sticking up in the air where they got him, a couple of bumps on his head, and his lip bleeding. He still had his cape, but his cape was ripped...and C. Archer was mad, because they are the

only ones that really took a stand. Tojo had fought them
off of him. They hadn't really gotten to Tojo. Polecat,
who is a hellcat, had left early. He didn't get involved. I
tried to get them to go home at about 10:30 because they
were disorganized. Some of them went home and some
were mad enough to go to K-Town. Tommy Lee went to
K-Town and got shot at a couple of times. He ran out into
the middle of the street and ran down cars and then made
a break and let open on them with his shotgun. He didn't
hit them, but he shot at them. It was too far away for a
sawed-off shotgun. One thing…maybe the reason Tommy
Lee broke was because he ran to get his shotgun. After he
got his shotgun, he stood over there and watched. They
talked about him that night. But, they didn't just talk
about him; they talked about a lot of studs. The only ones
they didn't talk about were Calloway, C. Archer, Junior,
Tojo, and Big James. They didn't talk too much about
Billy. Billy got a club and was talking loud, but he didn't
hit anybody. He stayed in the middle of the street so that
he could break, stand off, and wolf at them. They went
there sober that night, because they didn't want to get
strung up. (Detached Worker Report, Dryden, March 9,
1961)

Another worker's report of the same incident provides additional
information, including (1) interaction between the Vice Lords who had
been fighting and those who had missed the fight and (2) reactions of
some of the Midget Imperial Chaplains who had witnessed the Vice
Lords "get a good butt whipping" by the Cobras:

Friday the 24th, I went up to the Elks and was met by George
Dryden and he told me to keep my fellows to the side, because
there was going to be a humbug between the Cobras and the
Vice Lords. George got the Cobras and the Vice Lords
together and was talking to them, trying to talk them out of
whatever they were going to do. When he brought both of
them together…both were the heads, Stumpdaddy and Tommy
Lee. All of a sudden, they just got to the point where they
started arguing and in the big crowd like this they started

yelling. Chairs started flying and bottles and everything else. So, I grabbed as many of my fellows as I could and told them, "Let's stay to the side and play spectator and watch the fight." The protective detectives that were working at the Elks Hall cleared the hall and I immediately took my boys on the other side of Ogden and we watched. There was complete chaos up and down two blocks of Ogden Avenue. There were about 12 or 13 fights going on at once. They had weapons. I understand they were hidden somewhere, but they weren't able to get to them, because there were plainclothes detectives in the street and there were a few shots fired by the detectives just to stop some fights. But then, when they'd stop one, another one would break out 50 or 60 feet away. George and I were running around breaking up fights. Most of the Vice Lords had sticks and all kinds of weapons. At about 11:00, the hawk patrol showed up and they scattered. It was only half the Vice Lords out there fighting. The other half were somewhere else and then about this time they all started walking up, the other half that weren't even on the scene when the fighting took place, and you got this mighty boo from the rest of the Vice Lords, "Ah, you jive studs. You lame boo boo boo boo. Where you coming from now? You missed the fight and it's all over." They went on to explain that they had gone to get some heat somewhere to come and help them out. Most of my fellows just hung around and talked to the Vice Lords and made comments about the Vice Lords having gotten their ass kicked tonight and they were so glad. Most of my fellows are hostile towards the Vice Lords anyway and they were glad to see the Vice Lords get a good butt whipping. They were outnumbered tremendously. I guess there were about 70 Cobras and about 15 or 16 Vice Lords. Nobody got hurt because they were broken up as quickly as they started. A guy would get in with five or six punches and that was it. The police came on, but actually everything was over. (Detached Worker Report, Brown, March 2, 1961)

Social pressure favoring violence often was quite explicit in confrontations between rival gangs. Gang members were expected to defend against a rival gang that challenged them (or, in Stumpdaddy's words, not "kiss [the other gang's] ass") and failure to do so would result in a loss of status, as happened to the Vice Lord gang as a whole after being defeated by the Cobras and to the individual members— such as Tommy Lee, etc.—who abandoned their peers. Furthermore, individual gang members could elevate their status by refusing to back down from violence with members of a rival gang, especially when they were at some type of unfair disadvantage. Individual gang members who "stood their ground" in the face of unfavorable numerical odds "gained a lot of prestige," for example, even in cases in which they had been "whipped" and the reputation of their gang as a whole suffered. The increased likelihood of violence in disputes between members of rival gangs, then, may be attributed in part to the fact that both gang and individual status often were at stake.

While disputes between members of rival gangs were more likely than other types of disputes to end in violence, non-violent resolutions occurred quite regularly (40.7%). The same situational factors associated with non-violent resolutions of territorial disputes—unequal armament, unbalanced numbers, fearsome reputation, and mediation— also increased the likelihood that violence would be avoided in non-territorial disputes between members of rival gangs. Note, however, that most such cases did not involve entire gangs; rather, they involved so-called "wolf-packing," in which smaller groups of rival gang members took it upon themselves to stir up trouble with the enemy. When rival gangs came together specifically to do battle, the situation often was more volatile, and even the potential for serious harm and the presence of a face-saving reason for retreat did not ensure a non-violent outcome. The aforementioned "humbug," which apparently was prearranged and was supposed to have involved more Vice Lords than the ones who actually participated, clearly illustrates the explosiveness of rival gang conflict.

Extra-group disputes, in which either the offender or victim was an individual with no known gang affiliation, were shown earlier to make up almost 40 percent of all disputes. This high rate of occurrence cannot be understood without reference to the Detached Worker Program. Detached workers associated with this program were to immerse themselves in the gang context and to limit delinquent and violent behaviors through the provision of legitimate activities. Gang boys thus were brought into contact with non-gang individuals to a much greater extent than they had previously experienced. One consequence of this was the creation of new opportunities for extra-group conflict to emerge.[41]

Although extra-group disputes occurred frequently, they typically resulted in violence only when they involved a gang member against a girlfriend, stranger, rival non-gang individual, or a relative or close associate of a rival gang member. Except for a few cases in which preexisting hostilities and/or intoxicants were involved, potentially violent encounters between a gang member and a person in a position of authority (e.g., detached worker, YMCA employee, police officer, etc.) rarely escalated into violence, especially of a serious type. Non-violent outcomes were more common in these types of disputes, mainly because of mediation. While gang members were likely to prevent their peers from acting violently toward their detached worker, generally expressing clear disapproval of such behavior, the workers themselves often intervened to prevent violence toward other authority figures. The latter also sometimes acted to prevent violence between a gang member and another person of authority.

Another important reason behind non-violent resolutions of such disputes was that deference often was shown by the gang members who were involved. The following incident, reported by the detached worker with the Vampires, is representative:

> The night that we were out South, everything was over and he [Clinton] came over there talking about how he wanted to fight, and I said, "Alright, if you've got to fight, let's go." "Oh, no, I can't be fighting you, Mitch. No, you're our sponsor. I can't be fighting you." I said, "Alright then, there ain't going to be no fight." (Detached Worker Report, Mitchell, July 26, 1960)

---

[41] Perhaps the high rate of extra-group conflict contributed to the unexpectedly low rate with which members in the same gang became involved in conflict with one another. That is, intra-gang members may have been replaced by outsiders as targets of challenges.

Here, Clinton of the Vampires backs down from a potentially violent dispute with Ed Mitchell, the detached worker assigned to his gang. The reason for backing down, he says, was that he just could not fight his sponsor. Gang boys knew that violence with their detached worker—and, to a lesser extent, other authority figures—was risky, not just because such behavior potentially would place in jeopardy a valued relationship and all attendant privileges but also because group norms clearly worked against it. Thus, gang members were more likely to withdraw from potentially violent encounters with authority figures, especially their detached worker.

When disputes occurred between individuals with no known gang affiliation, non-violent resolutions were likely (68.4%). This is because these types of disputes often emerged between adults whose role in the community was to prevent or stop violence (e.g., detached worker, police officer, etc.), and at least one party, if not both, was apt to back down before violence developed. When violence did occur among non-group disputants—adult strangers, lovers, and non-gang friends or relatives—mediation by the detached worker or other third parties was rare, making it unlikely that violence would be squashed.

In sum, these data enhance quantitative findings related to the influence of the offender-victim relationship upon both the occurrence and outcome of dispute-related incidents. Not only do they show how the introduction of detached workers into the social milieu of gang boys contributed to the high rate at which extra-group disputes emerged (and perhaps to the unexpectedly low rate at which disputes emerged between members of the same gang), but they also shed light on the reasons why theoretical expectations of dispute outcome based on the offender-victim relationship either were upheld or contradicted. Preexisting hostility and supportive group norms made violence most likely in disputes between members of rival gangs, particularly when entire gangs were involved. Notwithstanding such strong pressures in favor of violence, however, these disputes often had non-violent outcomes. Weaponry (unequal), number of co-offenders and co-victims (unequal), opponent reputation (fierce), and detached worker/third party behavior (mediation) were contributing factors. Each of these operated as a situational cue to gang boys that violence with a rival gang member potentially would be more costly than backing down. More specifically, they suggested to the boys a greater than normal possibility that violence would result in serious harm and/or social disapproval. Three of the four—the exception being opponent reputation—also provided them with an opportunity to back down without losing face. Compared to disputes between members of rival gangs, disputes involving other types of offender-victim gang relationships were much more likely to end non-violently. In these disputes, status concerns usually were not as striking, and it was common for circumstances to suggest that backing down was a more socially acceptable alternative to violence (such as when the external audience mediated or when a detached worker was involved) or that the physical and social costs of violence outweighed the social costs of backing down. When neither of these conditions materialized or were simply overlooked (frequently as a result of intoxicants or preexisting hostility), the likelihood of violence increased.

Victim Behavior

Both quantitative and qualitative data indicate that victim behavior often was critical to the occurrence and outcome of dispute-related incidents. The latter, however, more clearly illustrates the contribution made by victims to the initiation of disputes and offers greater insight into the reasons for and consequences of their behavior following either a provoked or unprovoked verbal attack by the offender.

While there was evidence of victims being the targets of wanton identity attacks in approximately 1 in 7 cases, disputes more frequently occurred as a result of the victim behaving in such a way as to elicit a sanction by the offender (39.1%).[42] An example of this process can be seen in a report made by the worker with the Egyptian Cobras of the following incident involving two of the boys he sponsored:

> After the ballgame on Tuesday night, I went toward the poolroom, and Sherman went towards his house. James L. asked me what time I was going home, and Brewer and them said they would be back. The rest of them stood around and talked the game over, and they talked about some pretty white

---

[42] This figure differs slightly from the figure shown in quantitative discussion of reason for dispute occurrence because it: (1) distinguishes between norm- and order-violations and (2) collapses categories (see STRT_NRM in Appendix A).

girl that was coming to the park when they were coming and leaving at the same time. At that time, Ike started to go and so I didn't say anything because it is usually talk. I said, "One of these days, you are going to get hung up in the park. There's too much crap going on with Negro fellows trying to talk to white girls. You know we are out of the damn area." Wardell got mad at him. He said that is too far from home. He isn't saying anything to a white girl. Maybe he'll say something like "there goes a white bitch" or something like that if she is over at Maxwell Street. But, if you are out of the area, you don't say anything. They will get their ass kicked for something like that, and they know it. Wardell was mad because it was too far to run home. We all could have taken an ass kicking for that because she was about (inaudible). She had these (inaudible) pants on. She was going to play tennis. He was calling her baby, calling her trick, and all that kind of stuff. I told him, "You aren't over in the Maxwell Street area." Wardell was mad. He didn't say anything. James said "baby," but he didn't say anything about no damn trick. She heard it and then he kept calling her a Sunday bitch. He said, "You Sunday bitch," and then she turned and looked. I know she saw my car and that was when Wardell got hot. Wardell told him he had better keep his mother-fucking mouth shut. (Detached Worker Report, Dryden, August 18, 1960)

In this incident, the potential for violence emerged as a result of the victim, Isaac, engaging in a behavior that the offender, Wardell, viewed as inappropriate and therefore deserving of reproach. Many other disputes were initiated in a similar way. In general, the victim would engage in some sort of anti-normative behavior, after which the offender punished the victim in order to maintain social control. Victim behavior, then, clearly was an important factor in the occurrence of dispute-related incidents.

With the exception of disputes in which the offender physically attacked the victim without warning because of a preexisting hostility and/or the influence of an intoxicant or in which one or more co-victims physically attacked the offender before the interaction sequence between the offender and victim ran its course, victim behavior also influenced dispute outcome. In some cases, the victim responded with physical violence to the offender's initial attack or at least with such apparent readiness to use violence that the offender backed down. These behaviors were most likely when the victim was armed, intoxicated, and/or supported by co-victims. In other cases, however, victim resistance in the form of threats, identity attacks, non-compliance, etc. directly provoked the offender and/or co-offender(s) to use violence. An observer's report of what he had been told about the following incident involving Jimmy of the Dukes provides an example of the contribution that victim resistance (to an offender's attempt at social control) made to the escalation of disputes:

> While we were at John's house, the boys talked for a good hour of the fights they had been in during high school. Jimmy told of an ex-girlfriend who could not stand fighting and would threaten to break up with him any time she saw or heard about him having been in a fight. Once, he was on the bus with her while the two guys in front of them were using foul language. Jimmy said he kept his temper and leaned over and quietly told the boy that he had his girl with him, so would they mind not using such foul language. He said they sarcastically agreed and then proceeded to use worse language than ever. "What was I going to do, John? I couldn't just sit there and let them use that language in front of her. Yet, she did not like me to fight. Well, finally, I couldn't take any more, so I threw one guy out the window of the bus and hit the other guy. She got up and got off the bus, saying she did not want to see me any more, and that's the way it used to go. Every time she saw me get into a fight, she would tell me to stop and then leave me." Jimmy commented that she was an "angel of a girl," and she was so nice he would not even think of "touching her." (Observer Report, Pope, September 20, 1959)

In the following excerpt, the detached worker for the Stateway Cobras reports an incident in which one of his boys, Bernard, beats a woman who did not give him a cigarette when he asks her for one and who perhaps insults him by telling him he is "too young to smoke":

Wednesday night at the Community Center, Bernard blew his top and this lady, about 21...who is a member of the community center's dramatic club...they were having dramatic club practice or meeting or whatever they call it, and she came out in the hall and that is the only organization that meets in the Community Center that is allowed to smoke in their meeting. Well, she came out in the hall and she was smoking. Bernard asked her for a cigarette. Now, I think he knew this lady or this girl, although he didn't know her very well. But anyway, she told him that he was too young to smoke and she had cigarettes, but she wouldn't give him one. Now, he had been drinking a little wine and his wine told him to slap her and he beat the hell out of her right there. Mr. Ford put him out of the Community Center and barred him until July, until he brings his mother up. (Detached Worker Report, Smith, January 25, 1960)

The following detached worker report of an incident involving members of the 80th and Halsted gang against some Negroes[43] shows how victim resistance after an identity attack by the offender contributes to the development of violence:

Saturday night, Jim A., Rick, Tom, Mulcahy, Jim O., Pat...I'm not sure if anyone else, but those got into it with 3 Negro youths between 78th and 77th on Halsted and they were all arrested. The arrested were Pat, Jim O., and Mulcahy. One Negro had his throat cut by Pat with a beer can opener and Rick punched another Negro and almost broke his jaw. This started when they drove...the white boys were driving south on Halsted, and the Negro boys were walking North, and Tom or Arnold yelled out, "Hey, black son of a bitch," and the Negroes stopped and yelled back at the car and then the car stopped and everybody piled out and they stood in the middle of the street for about 10 minutes arguing back and forth. Finally, Rick got tired of it and said, "Well, let's either fight or

---

[43] With the assistance of the Vice Lords' detached worker, the worker with the 80th and Halsted gang (Anderson) subsequently determined that the Negro boys involved in this incident were not members of the Vice Lords.

forget it," and this Negro turned on him real fast to find out who said it, and Rick hit him and then this big Negro, one of the Negroes, said "I'm from the West Side. I'm a member of the Vice Lords" and all this jazz, and all during this, I was parked at 80th and Halsted, so when I saw the blue lights go flashing up to the corner I made it. (Detached Worker Report, Anderson, June 14, 1962)

Another example of the effect of victim resistance following an identity attack (by the offender) is provided by a report made by the Vice Lord's detached worker of an incident involving Guy of the Midget Vice Lords and a Senior Vice Lord who ends up slapping him:

Friday was fairly quiet. Guy had a run-in with one of the older boys. There were a few blows passed, but as soon as Guy saw the opportunity, he retreated. This boy is in the Senior Vice Lords, but he is not a leader. Guy was sitting in the restaurant with his head in his lap. This kid has been complaining about serious headaches the past couple of weeks. He had a headache, and this boy kept saying he was drunk. When Guy finally got up and talked back to him, the boy slapped him. This other boy had been drinking. This happened just as I arrived. Guy left. I didn't see him, and I suspected he had gone home. Every time he has a run-in with somebody, he will go home and come back, so I expect he was going home after a weapon. I went to his house, and because I was driving I got there before he did, so I called him to the car, and he got in and we talked about it for a while, and he still insisted on going into the house. When he came out, I talked to him again. I made him promise me that he wouldn't go back to 16th. (Detached Worker Report, Walker, March 12, 1962)

Victim resistance following either an effort to maintain social control, an influence attempt, or an identity attack by the offender clearly provoked the offender to respond with violence in these and other cases. Contrary to the conclusion reached on the basis of statistical data, then, resistant victims are shown here to have played a key role in their subsequent victimization. A possible reason for this discrepancy was suggested earlier by the finding that offenders were likely to back down when victim resistance was intense and indicative of a high potential for serious violence. More important, however, were subsequent actions taken by the victim and/or members of the external audience. Detached worker and third party mediation will be discussed at a later point.

Just as a resistant victim could contribute to the escalation of a dispute into violence, an obsequious victim could avoid impending violence altogether, at times even counteracting the effect of previous resistance. Offenders virtually never attacked a victim who offered an account or performed any other type of aligning action (87.4%), except when they were intoxicated and/or influenced by preexisting hostility. Victims were inclined toward such behavior primarily when the offender demonstrated a clear willingness to engage in violence. An observer's report of a dispute that emerged between Willy and Danny at a South Side Cobra dance offers an example:

> Ross and I arrived about 7:30 and began arranging the large room in which the dance was to be held. David came in with records and began to set up the record player for the dance. Tommy and another youth helped us straighten up the place. A little later, Shark came in and solo danced at times. Ross introduced me to Glen, the person in charge at the Y. After everything was set up and the record player was in order, the boys left to "get ready" for the dance. By getting ready, it appears as though they meant to get a drink or two. Ross, Mike, and myself talked on the outside for something like an hour before the youth began to arrive in groups of three to five. Ross introduced me to several of the youth, including Willy. Willy was collecting money and acting as doorman, "dressing" the fellows down as they came in to see if they had any weapons. Two girls helped Willy collect the money as the youth came to the top of the stairs. As the night went on, it was evident by the paid attendance that more than 105 youth attended the dance. Perhaps the average number there at any one time from 10:00 on was not less than 70. The youth would go in and out, and it appeared as though when they went out they frequently went to get something to drink. As the night moved on, the boys appeared to get higher and higher. In particular, I noticed a gradual change in Willy, Shark, and

David as they became increasingly intoxicated. Willy was going to be sure that no one got in without paying. Several youth, including Danny, attempted to get in without paying. Danny slipped in and stood in the corner for some time and Willy went over and asked him to pay his money. Danny refused. Willy asked, "What do you want me to do? Do you want me to hit you? Do you want me to hit you?" Finally, he got Danny to give him some money. I don't know how much it was. It cost 35 cents to come in, and whether Danny gave him the full amount, I am not sure. However, everything appeared to be all right between them. Another youth came in without paying and Willy tried to get him to pay. The youth refused and within a matter of seconds they were on the floor scuffling. The fight appeared to begin with a sort of horseplay, which crystallized into sharp opposition and conflict. The fight was quickly stopped by Ross and other youth who were repeatedly saying to the fighters, "be cool, be cool, be cool." (Observer Report, Moland, July 14, 1961)

A report made a few days later by the detached worker for the South Side Cobras provides further information about the incident:

Friday night was the Cobras' dance at the YMCA. Between the hours of 9:00 and 10:00, a hundred people came, all Cobras. Everyone in that place was a Cobra or a girlfriend of a Cobra. I think the ratio was maybe three to one, three boys to every girl. I do know that there was a fifth of vodka involved between Willy and Tommy, David, Fish, and somebody else. They drank it before they got in. Willy got drunk. He was very antagonistic. He was picking at people consistently. He was exercising his authority and showing his strength—Great Willy. Most of the kids there were afraid of him. (Detached Worker Report, Ross, July 19, 1961)

The importance of aligning actions in the squashing of violence also can be seen in the following detached worker report of an incident involving one of the Vampires (Harold) and one of the Vangales (Robert):

Both groups [Vangales and Vampires] claim to be the cheese group at the present time. Tuesday night, this situation was almost brought to a head in that the Vangales were practicing their singing at Steward Park and several of the Vampires, including Harold, Mack Roach, Hampton, Marcus, Hound, and several others, were in the room listening to them jam, along with several girls and also some off brand fellows who hang around Stewart Park. The five boys singing included Joe, who is the leader as far as the group is concerned singing-wise, a boy they call Squirrel, who is their second, also Meathead, and their bass, whose name is Robert. When Harold came in, he was a little high. The group was singing and accidentally he stepped on the bass's foot. Evidently, he [the bass player] had corns and he got mad and told Harold that, if he did it again, he was going to slap him down, in so many words. Harold apologized and asked forgiveness and everything was cool. (Detached Worker Report, Mitchell, April 21, 1960)

Although the potential for violence was evident in the disputes presented above, victim acquiescence in each case appeared to prevent an angry offender from engaging in a physical attack. In the first incident, Danny of the South Side Cobras (victim) attempts to get into the dance without paying the entrance fee and, consequently, is sanctioned by Willy (offender), also of the South Side Cobras. Initially, Danny refuses to comply with Willy's demand that he pay the fee, but upon realizing the seriousness of Willy's threat to use violence, Danny acquiesces and pays Willy the full amount or at least enough to pacify him. In the second incident, Robert (offender) sanctions Harold (victim) for stepping on his foot and threatens to use violence if it happened again. Harold immediately offers an apology, thereby preventing the dispute from escalating. Conciliatory measures such as those taken by Danny and Harold often were critical to non-violent dispute outcomes and, as shown here, were apt to occur when the offender demonstrated a clear intent to engage in violence.

In addition to an apparent readiness for violence on the part of the offender, a number of other conditions were conducive to victim acquiescence. The incident between Willy and Danny hints at one of these, which is the reputation of the offender. Victims were likely to offer an account or otherwise engage in an aligning action when the offender had a widespread reputation for violence, as did "Great Willy." Although not evident in the excerpts above, victims also were likely to submit when they were at a numerical or weapons disadvantage or when their antagonist was an authority figure or higher-ranking gang member.

Overall, both the descriptive and explanatory capability of these data advance understanding of the part played by victim behavior in the occurrence and outcome of dispute-related incidents. Disputes frequently emerged as a result of the victim behaving in such a way as to elicit a verbal punishment from the offender. Victim behavior following the offender's initial attack—whether provoked or not—also had important consequences. Because resistance represents a challenge to the offender's situated identity, such behavior generally increased the likelihood that the offender would respond with violence. Although this is contrary to the finding based on quantitative data that victim resistance significantly reduced the likelihood of a physical attack by the offender, consideration of the intensity of resistance as well as subsequent actions taken by the victim or members of the external audience permits reconciliation. Detached worker/third party mediation often was critical to the prevention of violence in disputes involving a resistant victim. Acute victim resistance (which occurred mainly when the victim was armed, accompanied by co-victims, and/or under the influence of intoxicants) also occasioned a non-violent response from the offender, as did the provision of an account or other aligning action by the victim following initial resistance. In fact, conciliatory measures were shown both here and in quantitative data to reduce the likelihood of offender physical attack in all cases, not just in those involving resistance. The implication is that victim acquiescence contributes to the squashing of disputes by counteracting any altercasting that has taken place or perhaps, in some cases, preventing its occurrence altogether. The decision to acquiesce generally was made by the victim when: (1) the offender-victim relationship suggested that backing down was more socially acceptable than violence or (2) the operation of other situational factors, such as unequal weaponry, unbalanced numbers, and offender readiness for violence, suggested that the potential physical and/or social costs of violence were high and that the social costs of backing down either were relatively low, if not nullified.

Detached Worker and Third Parties

The strongest theme to emerge from these data is the decisive role played by detached workers and other third parties in dispute resolution. As in quantitative data, disputes are shown here to generally have unfolded in a manner consistent with the expressed desires of the external audience. Conditions for active detached worker/third party behaviors are discussed, as are circumstances in which bystanders were influential.

Instigating behavior was most likely to occur when: (1) the third party was intoxicated; (2) one of the disputants was perceived by the detached worker or third party as a troublemaker and, therefore, deserving of a beating; and (3) the detached worker or third party was seeking entertainment in the form of a fair fist fight. This type of behavior, however, was shown earlier to be only rarely engaged in by third parties (5.6%) and even less frequently by detached workers (0.8%). In cases in which a detached worker or other third party did encourage the use of violence, disputants tended to behave accordingly, especially when they also were influenced by a preexisting hostility. A likely reason for this is that the maintenance of a favorable situational identity is contingent on doing what is expected by others. Non-violent outcomes, which were shown by statistical data to have developed much more often than not, may be attributable to the fact that mediation commonly mitigated against the amplifying effect of instigation, both when these behaviors were engaged in by two different people or groups[44] or when the same person or group engaged in the two behaviors at different points in time. The type of instigation (laughing versus clear agitation for violence) and the offender-victim relationship (gang member against detached worker versus gang member against rival gang member) also were important.

---

[44] This suggests that the effect of audience behavior varies according to the relationship between audience members and the target(s) of their efforts.

Protective or mediating[45] behavior, particularly by detached workers and peers (nearly always male), occurred much more frequently and was by far the most salient factor in the non-violent resolution of disputes. In general, detached workers were most likely to mediate when disputes jeopardized the use of a valued facility, involved intra-gang members or members of two friendly gangs, and/or seemed likely to escalate into serious violence (e.g., when weapons were present and/or when neither side of the dispute appeared to be backing down, often because of the influence of intoxicants).[46] This finding helps account for the unexpected negative relationship observed between dispute outcome and bystanding male youth (who typically were present during intra-gang and friendly inter-gang disputes) and between dispute outcome and victim resistance (which would signal to onlookers a high potential for the development of serious violence). Mediation by peers was most common during intra-gang disputes and disputes involving members of friendly gangs or their detached worker. The importance of the offender-victim relationship in the decision to mediate is shown in the following detached worker report of a dispute between members of two friendly gangs, the Vangales (Stacy) and the Vampires (Mack Roach):

> Anyway, an argument had started between Mack Roach [who was high] and another guy. I didn't know him. Stacy asked them to be quiet. They quieted down for a while and the argument re-ensued. Stacy then said, "Okay, everybody has to go. We want to clear the room." There were about 15 people in there altogether including myself and the singing group. So, they started to go out slow and Mack Roach was taking his time. He wasn't going fast enough to suit Stacy and so Stacy said, "That means you too" and started pushing and Mack said, "Say man, you don't want to be pushing on me. I'm

---

[45] Mediating behavior typically took one or more of the following forms: (1) physical intervention; (2) mention of potential formal and/informal sanctions, including disapproval; and (3) threatened loss of privileges, such as use of recreational facilities, attendance at special events, and help in the obtainment a job.

[46] On rare occasions, however, detached workers and third parties intentionally chose not to mediate due to their belief that intoxicants had eliminated the possibility that violence would result in severe injuries among disputants.

getting ready to go anyway." All this time, Harold was sitting in the back and he had made no effort to go. Stacy said, "You get the fuck on out of here because we want to practice and you're making too much noise." He said, "Man, you don't have to be pushing on me." He said, "I'll do worse than that. I'll pack you up and throw you out of here." Mack Roach kind of backed down. He's about 125 pounds and Stacy is packing 185 at least. So, they kept arguing and finally Mack Roach went out and all this time big boy Marcus (he knows both of them real well) said, "You got no use to be fighting over something like this. This is nothing, you understand. This might start something between the two groups and we supposed to be partners." I, too, was talking to both sides and telling Mack Roach to cool it and also Stacy. I don't know Stacy's group as well, but they want me to manage their singing group. So, we finally got the situation cleared up and fellows went back in to sing. I excused myself and stepped out to talk with Schoolboy who was also on the scene and a member of the Vampires, who had wanted me to help him get a car. I also talked to Mack Roach at the time and told him that in a way he was wrong and in another way Stacy was wrong in that Mack Roach wasn't the only one in there that was making noise. We got the situation smoothed over. As we were getting ready to...after the Vangales finished practicing, I went out and talked to Mack Roach and Stacy together and both of them were of the opinion that one was trying to mess over the other and he didn't want to get messed over and all that. I said, "Well, this was just a misunderstanding and the groups are too tight to be fighting over something like this. In a way both of you are wrong and you acted more or less like kids rather than men." I told them too that if the fight had started neither one of them would have won because the Vangales would have been kicked out of the park and couldn't use the room anymore and there would be continuous rivalry between the two groups which were really tight. So, Mack Roach got with Squirrel and a couple other Vangales. They went down to one of the local taverns, the Hi-Fi Club, and everything was forgotten as far as they were concerned. (Detached Worker Report, Mitchell, April 21, 1960)

Although protective/mediating behavior did not always result in non-violent dispute outcomes, such as in some of the cases involving a preexisting hostility, intoxicants, lackadaisical intervention, and/or contradictory behavior by the detached worker and third party,[47] it often did reduce the severity of violence or the occurrence of violence altogether. Disputes were most likely to be resolved non-violently when protecting/mediating behavior was engaged in by the detached worker or some other influential individual (e.g., high-ranking gang member, etc.) and/or was backed by a weapon (as was common with mediation by the police):

> There was a near fight with Kenneth and another guy who has the same type of personality. Before it got too far out of hand, I pulled Kenneth off. I have tried this on occasion and sometimes have been unsuccessful. He has a very aggressive...he has a chip on his shoulder and he wants to fight at the drop of a hat, and this man that he had words with was the same type of person, an older fellow who wouldn't take anything off one of these young punks. But, I got Kenneth off before any real harsh words developed. Kenneth wouldn't stand away from the table when this man wanted to shoot. I think they were playing quarter 2-pea, and Kenneth told the man to shoot, "I'm not moving." I could tell something could have developed, but I called Kenneth over to the side and said, "Why do you want to be like that?" and then we started talking about something else. But, this guy loves to humbug too. Last time this happened, Kenneth didn't pay any attention to what I was saying. He pulled away from me and Pop Sil had to pull his gun on him to break up this little humbug that was going to take place. But, this time, Kenneth did come over and listen to me. (Detached Worker Report, Gilmore, April 24, 1961)

---

[47] In these cases, either the detached worker or third party would accede to the other. The potential seriousness of the dispute appears to have been a key factor leading to the acquiescence of the mediating party to the encouraging party or vice versa.

The role of mediation in reducing the severity of violence can be seen in a report made by the Vampires' worker of the following incident involving Shane of the Midget Vampires against one of the fringe members of the Senior Vampires:

Everything went off fairly well at the canteen last night, although Shane bumped one of the fringe members of the Seniors. This is the same boy that wanted to get Shane's brother Monday. We broke it up before it got that far. He and this boy wanted to go. First thing Shane did was pull his shank. I talked to him and talked him out of it and he gave it to his girl. I said, "We don't want that play down here. We got a good thing going, and if somebody gets cut, I can't tell what is going to happen. The place will shut down and everybody will lose," and one thing he likes to do is dance. I said, "You've been having a ball here, and that would cut your ball out if you start something like that." I said, "Be a man and forget this thing." He said, "I am willing to forget, but those fuckers keep coming on back to me." I said, "I know, but he is a little bit high. Let me talk to him." I talked to Shane and I talked to the other guy [who is real tight with Freddie and Bird and that faction of the Seniors], and he said he was going to forget it. I didn't believe it, but I let them go their own way. They met just as they got out, and some words were passed and they started humbugging. Nobody got hurt. I don't think either one of them even got knocked down. We got to them before it got any worse. Shane was mad because he was being squared for the boys, and he is supposed to be the cheese. This would be a ticklish situation, because it would be the Midgets against the Seniors. Freddie came on the scene, and he accused Shane of having a shank in his pocket. I said, "There won't be any humbugging." I said, "Shane is clean. I got his shank. It was a fair fight, and they are willing to forget it, so let's get it over with." So, Freddie called his partner back and they shook hands and said they would forget it. (Detached Worker Report, Mitchell, January 12, 1961)

It is impossible to overlook the importance of mediation. In the incidents presented above, as in many others, mediation by the detached worker and mediation backed by weaponry were both particularly effective in squashing or minimizing violence, even when violence appeared likely and potentially severe. Although in the first excerpt the detached worker recalls a previous incident in which his attempt to mediate was unsuccessful, both these and statistical data indicate that mediation by detached workers more often resulted in non-violent outcomes (or a decreased severity of violence) than not. Furthermore, these data reveal a general awareness of the efficacy of such behavior, not only on the part of the detached workers themselves but also on the part of the gang members, who tended to avoid their worker when they were determined to engage in violence (for example, when they were seeking revenge) or other types of delinquency. Mediation by others did not occur to the same extent as mediation by detached workers, but when it did, violence was likely to be squashed, whether completely or only partially. Regardless of its source, then, mediation often was a key factor in the development of non-violent dispute resolutions or at least in the curtailment of the seriousness of any violence that did occur.

Depending on their characteristics or social status, bystanders sometimes were influential. The mere presence of individuals who occupied a position of authority and who were likely to disapprove of violence, such as a detached worker, police officer, local priest, etc., had a dampening effect on disputes.[48] In contrast, the likelihood and severity of violence was increased by the presence of individuals whom disputants wished to impress or in front of whom they did not want to look bad. The following incident involving Bobby and Richard from the Wolf Park area is apposite:

---

[48] The regular presence of detached workers during intra-group interactions and during disputes with male youth bystanders (36.6% of which were intra-group when disputes involving a participating detached workers are excluded) at least partly explains why disputes between members of the same gang were relatively infrequent and why non-violent dispute outcomes were more likely when disputes emerged in the presence of male youth bystanders than when other types of people were watching.

I didn't approach Wolf Park until last night. There was a goodly crowd there. I counted 22 boys. There was one girl. [Rich and Bobby had gotten into a fight because Rich had been coaxed by some of the other boys to go into one of his "trances," and in the process of acting like a gorilla-like creature, he had choked Bobby's girlfriend]. During the fight, Rich lost his shoe. None of the guys had his shoe, and Rich became quite upset. He said, "Where's my shoe? Damn it, it's around here someplace." Then, Rich said, "Well, I lost my cigarettes too." At about this time, Bobby had come out and sat down on the bench, and he had a pack of cigarettes. Rich happened to look over at on this table where this kid was sitting with two other guys, and he said, "Hey, you got my cigarettes. I lost them before when I was in the trance." Bobby said, "Naw, these aren't your cigarettes. These are my cigarettes." At this point, he began taking the cigarettes out of the package and destroying them, tearing them apart right in front of Rich. Rich said, "Those are my smokes." He said, "They're not your smokes." Rich said, "Give me my cigarettes." "I'm not going to give you your cigarettes." "I'm going to get them." Rich came at this kid, and he grabbed him by the hand, and Bobby was still kind of upset from the previous attack. He said, "Now, back off Rich. I don't have your cigarettes, and I don't like anybody breathing down my throat and calling me a liar." Rich wouldn't back off, and he wouldn't admit that it wasn't his cigarettes. He wanted those cigarettes, and that was it. So, finally, the kid said, "To hell with you, Rich. If you want to fight, let's go." He jumped off the bench and turned around. Rich said, "Yeah, I'll fight." He squared off, and they started throwing punches at each other. Rich did throw a few punches, but for the most part he would lower his shoulder and go in at the guy's midsection and upset him. So, they were wrestling all over the floor and getting up. It was a real nice brawl going on. Nobody tried to stop the fight. Finally, Bobby got Rich down and got on top of him. He had his shoulders down with his knees, and he asked Rich if he'd had enough, and Rich said yes. Bob was going to let him up, but after Rich said yes, that he had enough and wanted to call it quits, it seemed like Bob suddenly realized that he was

actually in the driver's seat, and he made a motion to lift his
knee as if he was going to get up and then he planted it down
firmly on Rich again and he started talking strictly for the
benefit of the guys watching, to the extent of saying, "Rich,
I've got you good. I'm in the driver's seat now, and I could
really beat the hell out of you. You'd better not mess with me,
because I'm a rough, tough SOB." He pounded his head a
couple times on the concrete floor to show that he was able to
do it without any resistance from Rich. While he was showing
off how rough and tough he was in the driver's seat, Rich
made a sudden move to get up. So, Bobby hit him a half a
dozen times in the face with his closed fist—real solid blows.
In fact, he knocked one of Rich's teeth out. Finally, Rich
stopped struggling, and he said, "Yes, I'm through. I'm
through." This time, Bobby did let him up. All the guys were
very much pleased to see Rich get beat up. I was surprised,
because they all recognize that he isn't all there mentally.
Some of the kids commented that he shouldn't be allowed to
walk loose, that he should be back at the hospital. (Detached
Worker Report, Lamotte, February 24, 1960)

In the next excerpt, the detached worker for the Nobles describes
an incident in which one of his boys, Bobby, gets into an argument
with his girlfriend and appears to be especially perturbed by the fact
that she was challenging him while his friends (male youth) were
watching:

Saturday evening, I went into the poolroom and Bobby asked
me if I was coming to the jam, and I asked where it was, and
he said, "My girl's." I said, "Yeah, I will come. Let me know
when you're ready to go." The guys started coming in the
poolroom. After the poolroom got crowded and the noise
picked up, Bobby's close associates, who he had invited to the
dance, started to play pool and take up on wine. This is all in
preparation of Bobby's party. During that evening, I would
say there were at least four fifths of wine bought. They were in
a loud vociferous mood by the time we got ready to walk on
over to the party. She lives directly across the street from the
poolroom. There were 4 or 5 girls there, but the fellows there

even turned their noses up at them. Bobby and his girlfriend, Juanita, almost got into a humbug while I was there. And, if anybody else would have tried to break it up, he would have hit her, but I don't think he wanted to hit her and show me he was wrong. They were arguing about something she had done. The more they argued, the louder they became, and this was really annoying him, the fact that she was standing up in front of him and in front of his friends. So, I told him, "Let's get out of here." It was about 12:00. "We'll go on back to the poolroom and shoot a couple quick games of pool before it closes." In the house, there were about 12 teenagers in there and there was wine, but nothing stronger than wine. It was a dirty, crummy house and this was another thing that got Bobby kind of annoyed. The fellows didn't act like they were enjoying it, and he called it his party, and they were making open comments about it. They were openly teasing Bobby about this person he was going with, her house, etc. He can roll with the punches, but it was getting to him and he might have tried to take it out on her to show them she didn't mean a damn thing to him. (Detached Worker Report, Gilmore, December 12, 1960)

At times, the presence of girls contributed to the occurrence of disputes and/or their escalation into violence, as in the following case reported by the detached worker for the Braves:

Thursday night, after the dance in Seward Park, there were at least six fights or more [involving members of the Braves against each other and against other people]. Started off with an argument between Richard and an older fellow from the South Side, a boy named Ray. Ray had been drinking and some of the Braves had been drinking. Three boys that hang with the Braves but aren't on my roster were stoned and were out. Guys that tried to stop the fights would get swung on accidentally and then they would get into it. Richard got into it with Tootsie later on. Snowball got into it with one of these boys that was high. Just one fight started another. You might say the climax was when these three men who live in the area tried to break some of it up, and they all wanted to jump on them. We were finally saved by those precious dogs from the canine corps. From 9:30 until about 12:30, I was stopping fights, one after the other, except for about 15 minutes when I took this fellow [Ray] who had gotten jacked up by Tootsie for a ride to cool him off. All the rest of the time, until the dogs came, I was breaking up one fight after another. I saw Sam the next day and he said he saw what was happening, and I said, "Why didn't you come out and help?" and he said, "There were 70 some of them drunk jokers out there and I wasn't going to get out there. I'd probably get jacked up myself." I said, "Why didn't you get your brother Hound, because Hound could have helped?" There must have been between 40 and 60 kids out there. Some of them were just showing off for the girls and others were just getting it off their chests. (Detached Worker Report, Mitchell, June 25, 1962)

Detached workers and observers often alluded to the possibility that dispute occurrence and outcome were influenced by the presence of certain bystanders. In the first incident presented above, the worker states that, toward the end of a brief scuffle, Bobby (non-gang) got on top of Rich (non-gang) and "started talking strictly for the benefit of the guys watching, to the extent of saying, 'Richie I've got you good. I'm in the driver's seat now, and I could really beat the hell out of you. You'd better not mess with me, because I'm a rough, tough SOB.'" He then proceeded to pound Rich's head on the concrete floor "to show that he was able to do it without any resistance." In the next incident, the worker suggests that, had it not been for his presence and mediating actions, Bobby surely would have hit his girlfriend, Juanita, because of the fact that she was standing up to him "in front of his friends." In the last incident, the worker attributes the development of violence at least partially to the desire on the part of some of the boys (Braves) to show off for the girls who were present.

In sum, these data are consistent with quantitative findings in that they show dispute outcome to be strongly influenced by audience behavior. However, these data also (1) provide insight into the conditions of each type of behavior, (2) offer reasons for variations in the statistical data, and (3) clarify findings related to the impact of bystanders. Instigating behavior was rare, occurring primarily when third parties were intoxicated, one of the parties to the dispute was perceived by the audience as deserving of a beating, or the audience wanted to witness a fair fist fight. While statistical data indicate that most disputes involving instigation did not escalate into violence, there is evidence here to suggest an amplificatory effect, particularly when preexisting hostilities also were operating. Factors contributing to non-violent resolutions included simultaneous or subsequent mediation, low intensity encouragement, and a detached worker-gang member offender-victim (or victim-offender) relationship. Unlike encouraging behavior, protective/mediating behavior occurred regularly, most often when disputes had a high potential for serious violence or jeopardizing the use of a valued facility or when they involved intra-gang members, members of two friendly gangs, or a detached worker against anyone else. The linkage between protection/mediation and non-violent dispute outcomes was perhaps the strongest finding in these data, though the effectiveness of protection/mediation was sometimes hampered by a preexisting hostility between disputants, intoxicants, and/or a contradiction in the actions taken by detached workers and other third parties. The effect of bystanders (though not strong) varied. Individuals in front of whom disputants wanted to look good and avoid looking bad (e.g., members of the opposite sex) contributed to violence, while authority figures generally contributed to non-violent outcomes. Disputes, then, were likely to unfold in a manner consistent with the admonitions of active third parties or with the values disputants sometimes imputed to non-active third parties on the basis of their demographic characteristics or social position. This suggests that disputants generally were concerned with the maintenance of an acceptable situated identity in front of an external audience. When third parties instigate or are perceived to approve of and/or expect violence, they place added pressure on disputants to resort to violence or risk losing face. Conversely, when third parties protect/mediate or are perceived to disapprove of violence, disputants risk losing face (and, at times, more formal sanctioning) if they do not back down but risk little to nothing if they do.

Intoxicants

Another prominent theme in these data is the importance of intoxicants, particularly alcohol and pills, in dispute-related incidents. In addition to revealing a neutralizing effect that intoxicants sometimes had on the factors that led frequently to non-violent dispute outcomes (e.g., outnumbering, unequal armament, certain types of offender-victim relationships, opponent who demonstrated apparent readiness to engage in violence, etc.), ample evidence supports the widespread assumption—by detached workers, observers, and dispute participants—that intoxicants were a major contributor to the occurrence and escalation of disputes. Belligerency and other testing behaviors were possible consequences of intoxication, as can be seen in following incident involving Little Pient against some of the Dukes:

> I think it was Saturday or Sunday night when Little Pient was three sheets to the wind. He had been drinking wine all evening. I was with a bunch of Dukes in my car, and we drove up to Rossi's and went inside and had our coffee and pizza. On our way out, Little Pient was standing out in front with Frank and Rich. I had five Dukes with me, and we climbed into my car, and as we started to drive away, the three guys naturally had to come over. They started talking to us, and Little Pient began rapping the Dukes. He was saying that the Dukes were a bunch of punks, no good young hoods, sissies, their club wasn't worth a damn, it was rated the lowest in the park area, and blah blah blah. The Dukes tended to see humor in the situation. They knew that Little Pient was drunk, and they kind of chuckled every time he said the Dukes were this and that. They were laughing and saying, "You're right, Pient." But, he became very heated in his remarks, and the guys began to see that Little Pient really meant what he was saying. So, some of the guys began to change some of their responses in the sense that they'd say, "What do you mean? Let's knock this out about the club. We got a good club, and we wouldn't want the likes of you in it" and so on. As a result, Little Pient became very hostile and took off his jacket, and he said, "I'll challenge every Duke in this damn neighborhood to fight here and now." So, the guys kidded him a while about that, but he kept insisting that he could beat up any Duke in

the area, and Little Bobby reached the end of his line, you might say, and he said, "Let me out of this damn car." So, he jumps out of the car and goes up to Little Pient and says, "All right, you've been rapping the Dukes, and you can't take it yourself. If you want to fight, let's go." Little Pient had worked himself up into a lather by now, and he was waving his fists in the air and he said, "You symbolize all the Dukes to me. I'll pounce on you as anyone else." So, they decided to go to the parking lot, which is right next door to Rossi's. The rest of us trailed over behind them. I made no effort to intervene. The boys are more or less evenly matched; they're the same size. By this time, Little Pient seemed to have overcome this drunken state, and he seemed to know what he was doing, so I felt that he was capable of taking care of himself in a fight. Anyway, the two boys got out in the parking lot and were sparring around, throwing jabs that did not hit. They were about three feet from each other, but they were going through the motions of having a fight. Then, one of the older guys, who's about 30 and who works at Rossi's, stepped between the two youths, and that ended the fight. We then moved back to the street in front of Rossi's. Little Pient put his jacket back on, and we all got back into the car. There were a few more remarks to the effect that "Anytime you want to fight, Pient" or "Go to it" or "Let's go down to the park." So, Bobby suggested that they go down right then and there, and Little Pient said, "Hell no, I'm still half stiff, but I'll catch you tomorrow night when I'm sober. I'll stand a better chance." That was the parting remark, and we drove off in my car. Pient was rapping the Dukes so badly that Bobby felt that he had to defend the honor or reputation of the club. They talked about Pient, about the way he was bum rapping the club. Some of the kids kind of admired his guts, because on this particular night Pient had stood up to what could have been six or seven guys. They passed it off as the liquor talking, but they were surprised and kind of put him one step higher in their estimation, because he was really willing to take on the entire Dukes. (Detached Worker Report, Lamotte, December 16, 1959)

In other cases, consumption of intoxicants negatively affected an individual's ability to behave in a socially acceptable manner. Excerpted from a report made by the detached worker with the 80th and Halsted gang, the following incident involving Jim and a "doped up" Ward provides an example:

Ward did have a fight with Jim Monday night, and being so doped up, he did surprisingly well. I let him only go about five minutes. At first, I tried to stop it, but Ward didn't even go five minutes. (inaudible) in the group were saying, "Stay out, let him go." Finally, I said, "That's enough of this shit. Stop it." This was in Kroeger field. One punch knocked Jim out. This was over Ward dropping his trousers when Jim and Jim's girlfriend were walking by. He pulled them back up, and the guys all laughed, and Ward deliberately pulled them down again. Jim said to Ward, "Don't do that in front of my girl," and Ward said, "Why not?" Jim said, "It's not right," and Ward said, "What are you going to do about it?" Jim had little choice but to fight, and Jim you could tell was a bit afraid...and Ward was happy when I stepped in, because he was tired at this point. (Detached Worker Report, Deering, June 9, 1961)

Reporting on what the worker had told him about the same incident, an observer states:

Ralph asked about the fight last night, saying he was not close enough to see what was going on. Lee told him about the fight, as he had told me earlier. Jim walked up with his girl and Ward went over in front of her and pulled his pants down and then pulled them up again. The guys laughed, so Ward did it again. West told him to cut it out, that it was his girl, and not for him to do that in front of her. Ward asked him why not and Jim repeated because it was his girl. Ward asked him, "What the fuck are you going to do about it?" and at this point Jim, seemingly reluctant but feeling he had to show he was a man in front of his girl and the group, joined Ward in fight. Lee let them fight a while and then broke it up. Lee said it was just a little fight for a while and no one won. Lee said Ward did pretty well for a guy who was high and that Ward must be quite a fighter when he is not high. (Observer Report, Pope, June 6, 1961)

Consumption of intoxicants also adversely affected individuals' ability to deal non-violently with infractions on the part of others. In the following excerpt, the detached worker with the Sub Grill gang describes an incident in which intoxicants appear to have diminished one of his boy's tolerance for a minor impropriety on the part of some other boy who frequented the Sub Grill establishment:

Friday night, I was talking to Mary [in the Sub] when there was a commotion outside. When I went out there, the kid was down. Tony picked the kid up. He went over to Don and was arguing with Don when I came out. I saw him take a swing at Don. Of course, I threw my arms around him and pulled him away. Don didn't know what to do. They all respect Tony and he respects him, too. Don was high and Tony said, "You got a few drinks in you and you think you're God almighty." When I was pulling Tony back, Tony said, "Bob, wait a minute. He hit that kid because he stepped on his shoe. You ever hear anything so goofy? He cracked him because the guy stepped on his shoe, and he didn't apologize to him." Don had walked in and called the kid out. Finally, I got Tony cooled off and got him in and went across the street and said, "What happened?" So, Don told me what happened. Guy just stepped on his shoe. I said, "What kind of reason is that for belting the kid? You were drinking." "No, I wasn't." "Wait a minute. Don't lie to me. You were drinking." I said, "You know that every time you drink this happens. One more fight you're in and there will be no more boxing." Then, I saw Tony coming across the street. I said, "Simmy, you stick with this guy. Cover him like a blanket. Take him for a walk around the block or something. I want to talk to you again." So, I went and grabbed Tony and said, "Come on Tony, let's go in for coffee." Tony wanted to get back at him again he was still so mad. I told him..."I know he's high and he doesn't know what he's doing. What good is it going to do him to crack him now? You know he's not like that when he's sober. If he would have done something like this when he was sober, I would have given him a crack myself." Tony knew the boy because he's a regular customer there. So, that was it. I had forgotten about it, but Don told me the next day that when he cracked the guy, Wayne gave him a few kicks. (Detached Worker Report, Jemilo, October 25, 1960).

An excerpt from the observer's report provides the following supplementary information:

Bob came into the Sub Grill. I sat at the table while most of the group sat at the bar. Bob sat in one corner talking to Mary, the proprietress of the place. Don came briefly in and motioned for a younger guy of about 15 to step outside and proceeded, with Wayne's help, to beat the guy up. As usual in cases like this, most of the group went outside to watch... including most of the girls. The place was almost deserted before Bob realized that something was up. He noticed that I was about to go outside and asked me whether I was leaving, so I walked over and told him it would be a good idea for him to be outside. Don was saying to the kid when I went out, "Next time don't step on my shoes when you come into this place." The kid was on the ground, and Don was standing over him. Bob walked up at the same time that Tony, the proprietor of the Sub Grill, went outside. Tony was extremely angry at Don and started to fight with him. Bob stepped in between Tony and Don. Tony was disturbed that Don would give the place a bad name and that the kids from Waller would cease to come into the place because they would be afraid of being beaten up. He was also angry because Don had been drinking. He said that this always happens on Friday, that he has too much to drink and then he comes in bothering someone. Bob kept having to keep Tony away from Don. Eventually, Bob got Don to go across the street and Tony to stay on this side. The other members of the group stood at a fairly safe distance and watched this occurrence, none of them really angry at the situation. (Observer Report, Freedman, October 14, 1960)

The contribution made by intoxicants to the escalation of disputes into violence is also shown in the following detached worker report of an incident between Little Joe and Freddy:

> After the game Friday, my boys dressed and we went over to the Elks Hall, where they have their dance every Friday night. There was one incident between two Imperials, Little Joe and Freddy. I don't know what the fight really started over, but all I could see was that Little Joe had been drinking and was angry because Freddy had said something to him, some smart remark, which probably wouldn't have started a fight if Little Joe hadn't been drinking. I stopped this fight before it became an actual battle. It was just a couple of licks. I held Little Joe. Freddy was content not to fight, but he was not backing down. He would have fought if Little Joe had pushed on and kept the fight going, but I held them off and Joe's girl took him home and Freddy went on his way with the rest of the group. That night, drinking wasn't evident, but you could tell that they might have been drinking, but not heavy drinking. Little Joe was about the main one that I thought had been drinking quite a bit. (Detached Worker Report, Brown, January 20, 1961)

Worker and observer reports indicate that intoxicants predisposed individuals to engage in both confrontational and norm-violating behaviors and to react violently to the transgressions of others, thus offering a potential explanation for the high proportion of disputes involving intoxicants (97.4%) and for the statistical relationship between intoxicants and escalation of disputes into violence. The incidents presented above are cases in point. By adversely affecting Little Pient's (non-gang) and Ward's (80th and Halsted) behavior, intoxicants (alcohol and pills, respectively) contributed to the development of the dispute with the Dukes and the dispute with Jim. The influence of intoxicants also may have contributed to both boys' willingness to respond with violence to those who chastised them. In the two latter incidents, intoxicants appear to have temporarily impaired the ability of Don (Sub Grill) and Little Joe (Junior Imperials) to deal non-violently with what they perceived to be inappropriate behavior on the part of others. Had they been sober, the workers suggest, it is unlikely that the disputes would have escalated.

Intoxicants also appeared to increase the likelihood and severity of violence through their impact on victim resistance. An apposite case is an incident in which the South Side Cobras' worker gets into a brief wrestling match with Willy, who ordinarily was more respectful:

> Friday night, there was a dance at the South Town YMCA given by a Hi-Y club, girls Tri-Hi-Y club, which constitutes about 50 of the Cobraettes. Present were all my boys, about 80 of the Cobras in the area, plus 7 boys representing the K-Town Cobras and 4 Hyde Park Devil's Disciples. The dance went along pretty good until Willy got high and started shaking down some of the kids. We had a few words about it and I started out with an argument with me to quiet him down. He took a package of cigarettes from Deedee, and we wrestled, and I tore his coat, and that was when I decided I had better leave him alone before we started to really get into it good. (Detached Worker Report, Ross, March 22, 1961)

A report made by the Playboys' worker of the following incident involving Jim and some police officers provides another example:

> Friday, the most notable thing was that the Playboys had a dance at Taylor House. The fellows had been drinking prior to the dance. I was in the House and John went outside. I didn't realize this at the time, until Dottie, who is a worker at Taylor House, came and said the police were on the corner with John and asked if there was anything I can do about it. So, I went over there and was talking to one of the officers. John was pretty well drunk, mellow. He had gone into the tavern on the corner and tried to get served, and when they wouldn't serve him, they came out and he was going to throw something in the window, so one of the guys came out and knocked him over the head with a bottle, so he was bleeding and crying a little and was worried about being picked up on violation of parole. I got the officer outside and told him that John was involved in this manslaughter and was on five years probation and I was wondering if I took him with me, if he would let the charges go. The officer said this would be all right, so I took John with me and went back to Taylor House and at this time

there was another disturbance at Taylor house, and there were about 7 policemen in the house. I got John in the washroom and heard comments by some of the other guys, like "Son of a bitch John. He screwed up on us and he brings the police around because of his goofing off." A little later, I found out that the police had Danny, Mitch, and Jim. The reasons behind it, I'm not too sure, except I know the boys had been drinking. The police started to walk out with Mitch and Jim. Jim wanted to know why they were taking him in, and the officer said something about "because you're a punk." There was an officer in front of Jim and Jim said to him, "You mother fucker, you're not too..." The officer turned around and was quite heated. Jim was going to swing at him when another officer grabbed him in the neck and held him, and Jim started to kick. So, 5 officers carried him out, one on each leg and a couple on arms. They carried him to the wagon and Mitch walked out along side. I think it was the part of the police to show authority. All through the dance there was this big (inaudible) against John. I questioned some of the fellows and they were drinking wine and Vodka. There was no evidence of pot. John had been using pills. I am inclined to think they were high on drink, although I'm not positive. (Detached Worker Report, Bach, March 30, 1962)

The next excerpt contains an incident that developed in the police station after some of the Junior Valiant Gents had been arrested for fighting some other boys and for hitting a police officer when he tried to intervene:

They said the police came in there and took off their guns, and one police officer took off his shirt [he's a pretty big guy] and came in and started knocking them down, dared them to fight them back, and so forth, and they said they beat Son pitiful, because he wouldn't give them any type respect. The man would say something to Son and the Son told him to "kiss my ass" or something. He didn't have any win, but he was still fighting. Bernard said every time the police would walk toward him, he would put his hand over his face, and the man would tell him to put it down and he wouldn't put it down, and then he would smack him anyway. He was putting his hand over his face to protect his face and eyes. He didn't want the man to hit him in his eyes. (Detached Worker Report, Gilmore, June 28, 1962)

In these incidents, as in many others, resistance (physical or otherwise) on the part of the gang boys who were under the influence of intoxicants appeared to have provoked their opponents to respond with force. While we cannot be certain of how Willy (South Side Cobras), Jim (Playboys), and Son (Junior Valiant Gents) would have acted had they not been intoxicated, the data strongly suggest that intoxicants were at least part of the reason for their resistance, even mitigating against the influence of the offender-victim relationship (i.e., a person of authority against a gang member).

Although there is a clear link between intoxicants and violence, non-violent resolutions to disputes involving intoxicants either were more (61.2% of all cases in which only one party was under the influence) or at least equally (49.7% of all disputes in which both parties were under the influence) common. Provided that consumption of intoxicants did not preclude disputants' ability to behave in a manner that was rational given the presence of certain situational cues, unequal armament or imbalanced numbers, a close offender-victim relationship, and an opponent who demonstrated a clear readiness for violence all decreased the likelihood of a violent dispute outcome. Other relevant factors include: (1) the perception by one party that the other party was too intoxicated to fight and (2) detached worker and/or third party mediation.

At times, potential violence was squashed when one party of a dispute, whether intoxicated or not, withdrew because the other, intoxicated party was perceived as being in no condition to fight. Not only did the beating of such a person hold a low potential for status returns (unless the audience clearly was in favor of violence, such as in cases involving a member of a rival gang or of a different race), but such action also could backfire and result in a loss of face:

The big night was Saturday night...Halloween. We stayed in the poolroom until approximately 9:00. When they got ready to leave the poolroom, Thumbdaddy came up to me and seriously said that they were going to a dance at 3800 Lake Park and I was perfectly welcome to come along with them. I told them that I'd be out a little later. I left the poolroom and was on my way to the dance at 38th and Ellis when I ran into Lonnell, Al, Kenneth, and Chicken Hawk. I got in the car and drove over to 36th and Ellis, near the poolroom. [After we] left 36th and Ellis...we proceeded back to 36th and Cottage Grove, where I ran into Lonnie walking down the street with two quarts of beer. As soon as he saw me, he started to explain that the beer was not his, but was bought for the girls at the party at 611 E. 36th Street. I thought I'd better escort him over, and when I got there, I found William and Chicken Hawk standing in the hallway trying to get in. It was an invitation only party. Al went with me. Kenneth went with me. He had an invitation. Kenneth and Lonnie went in. Thumbdaddy was already in the party and the girl still wouldn't let William and Al into the party, so they were standing in the hallway creating a disturbance. So, I just pulled them out and told them to wait, and I went down and met the parent...and the kids were in the front room with no lights hardly whatsoever. Teenagers...they were sitting around. They had smuggled the bottles in, and they were drinking. Everything looked pretty peaceful, so I took off and left there. In the meantime, Chicken Hawk was insulted because he couldn't get into the dance and he was going to catch his bus and go down to 46th and Greenwood to a party that he was invited to. While waiting on the corner, a drunk came up to him and started to ask him directions and make himself obnoxious and Chicken Hawk just turned around and hit the guy in the mouth, before anybody could stop him. The poor drunk got up and ran away, and we stopped Hawk and his chest stuck out like he was a martyr or something, like he'd done something so great. Actually, he had cut his hand all up and it was really a bad cut. He [the drunk] was drunk and so the boys ridiculed him for hitting the drunk like that. So, he said, "later," because he was going on off. (Detached Worker Report, Ross, November 4, 1959)

Individuals could jeopardize their status by directing violence toward an inebriated person. In the incident presented above, Chicken Hawk (Nobles) clearly expects to be rewarded with status from his peers after knocking the drunk fellow down, but his peers instead "ridiculed him for hitting the drunk like that." Disputants in cases such as these, then, were more apt to withdraw because the intoxication of their opponent meant that violent behavior not only would result in little to no gain in status but also would result in a loss.

Mediation was the most important reason for non-violent resolutions of disputes involving intoxicants. Although the effectiveness of mediation in preventing or stopping violence in these (and all other types of) disputes depended to a certain extent on who was doing it and how it was done, escalation typically was avoided when a detached worker and/or any other third party intervened.

Overall, these data make clear the importance of intoxicants in dispute-related incidents. The occurrence of disputes and their outcomes appear to have been directly affected by the contribution made by intoxicants to the development of confrontational and norm-violating behaviors and to a reduced tolerance for any such transgressions on the part of others. Intoxicants also contributed to the escalation of disputes through their impact on victim resistance. However, when either or both parties of the disputes felt that backing down was less costly than fighting, the amplificatory effect of intoxicants on dispute outcome tended to be mitigated. This was most likely when circumstances suggested one of the following options: (1) risk losing status by resorting to violence versus risk nothing by backing down (e.g., extremely intoxicated opponent, offender-victim relationship, or mediation); (2) risk serious physical injury and, depending on such factors as one's performance, either lose or gain status by resorting to violence versus risk nothing by backing down (e.g., outnumbered or out-armed); and (3) risk serious physical injury and, depending on such factors as one's performance, either lose or gain status by resorting to violence versus risk losing face by backing down (e.g., opponent readiness for violence). Although intoxicated individuals did not always accurately perceive or accede to situational cues favorable to non-violent resolutions, both these and quantitative data indicate that in many cases they did.

Weapons

Quantitative data indicate that the introduction of weapons into a dispute, regardless of whether it was done by only one party or by both parties, increased the likelihood of a violent outcome. As shown here, however, the weapon effect was much more complicated (and contingent on the operation—or lack thereof—of other situational factors) than is suggested by this finding.

Violence occurring during disputes in which only one party was armed resulted primarily from use of weaponry as a means of self-defense or retaliation (frequently by members of one gang upon a member or members of a rival gang). In these latter cases, violence often was based on an element of surprise, thus giving the victim little or no time to react prior to being attacked by the armed offender. The implication of this finding is that quantitative data may overstate the influence of weapons in the unfolding of disputes, as weapons may have been more important in determining how (easily) violence was carried out by people intent on doing so than in determining whether or not it would be (see Mullins et al. 2004; cf. Wells and Horney 2002). Even when the unarmed party was given more time to respond to the advancement of the armed party, weapons did not contribute directly to violence. Escalation of these disputes typically occurred in one of the following ways: (1) the unarmed party physically attacked the armed party before the latter had the opportunity to engage in a weapons attack or after the weapon proved to be faulty or was perceived to be incapable of inflicting real damage due to the intoxication and/or apparent lack of skill on the part of the wielder; (2) the unarmed party was intoxicated and/or unaware of the fact that the other party was armed and thus engaged in a physical attack or behaved in such a way as to provoke a weapons or non-weapons attack; (3) the unarmed party overpowered the armed party, taking the weapon (usually not a firearm) away and engaged in a physical attack with or without it; or (4) the armed party was outnumbered and attacked by the unarmed party. With the exception of disputes in which an armed party attacked an opponent who was unarmed but who resisted (usually while under the influence of intoxicants and/or unaware that the other party was armed), violence most often was initiated by the unarmed party. As indicated above, the unarmed party tended to attack when situational cues suggested that there was little to no risk in doing so or when perception of the risk was limited, perhaps because of incomplete information or intoxication.

Non-violent outcomes were less frequent in these types of disputes, but they did occur regularly (Possession = 37.8%; Threat = 46.1%). While mediation by a detached worker and/or some other third party was the most common reason for the avoidance of violence, submission by one party of the dispute was likely to generate the same outcome. Such behavior developed only under a limited set of conditions, however.

The first condition involves the relative number of participants on each side of the dispute. When one party, whether the armed or unarmed, was outnumbered by the other, submission was likely. Submission resulting from a deficiency in terms of numbers can be seen in a report made by the Nobles' detached worker of an incident involving a few of the Nobles against an older neighborhood male. Note that, in this case, as in all others in which the armed party backed down from a numerically superior opponent, the weapon involved was not a firearm.

> Sunday morning, we had a baseball game in Jackson Park between John Lamotte's Dons or Dukes and the Nobles. The Nobles got clobbered 24 to 4. There was almost a humbug at the game. Lamotte's manager, Larry, is about 22, a real wise guy. Wallace threw a bat (inaudible) accidentally. He was umpiring the game. He is real fair in his umpiring, I will have to give it to him. And, it hit him on the shin and he picked up the bat and went down the line and told Wallace if he ever did that again he was going to take that bat and wrap it around his ears and Wallace came off the base with Bobby and about three or four more Nobles and said, "Oh yeah, who in the hell do you think you are? You are not going to wrap that bat around anybody's ears, no matter what happens out here, and that goes for you and for everybody else out here." I didn't say a thing and neither did Lamotte…just sat there and looked at them to see how far it would go. So, Larry turned around and walked away, and Wallace and Bobby laughed. (Detached Worker Report, Ross, June 2, 1960)

One month later, the detached worker with the Sub Grill gang reported a similar incident involving Chips against some of the other members of his (Sub Grill) gang:

> The other night, about half an hour after the baseball game, when Chips had missed so many fly balls in the outfield, they were really down on him. He would make an error and they would chase Chips with a bat, kind of jokingly, until it finally burned him so bad that he finally went and got a bat himself and came back in the group swung it around and you could tell he looked like a rainy day. He was mad, but he finally knew there were too many, and he smiled and then it all broke up. (Detached Worker Report, Powell, July 1, 1960)

Although Larry and Chips were armed, they both backed down from an unarmed opponent upon realizing that they were outnumbered. Thus, even when disputants were armed with such weapons as baseball bats, they were likely to submit to their unarmed opponent if the latter was numerically stronger.

Submission also was influenced by the armament disparity itself. An example is shown in an observer's report of the following incident in which an aggressive male withdraws from a potentially violent confrontation with Bobby after Bobby threatens him with a chair:

> At a dance once, Bobby said that one of the older fellows told him to "move, punk." Bobby said "I picked up a chair and said, 'move me.'" The guy backed down and nothing happened. (Observer Report, Pope, September 15, 1959)

The detached worker with the Egyptian Cobras describes another case in which weapons are critical to the development of a non-violent outcome:

> On Sunday, I found out that on Saturday night one of the reasons Henry, Willie, and Wardell left the West Side so quickly was the fact that they had run into some of the Vice Lords at this restaurant. They meet the girls at this restaurant. At least some boys who had identified themselves as the Vice Lords...I don't know definitely whether they were or not.

> Henry, Willie, and Wardell had met these boys and these boys had told them, "We have enough of your coming around this area. You're going to stay out from now on or we'll fight." I understand that the boys had some shotguns and they really meant it. So, consequently, Henry and Willie left quite hurriedly. (Detached Worker Report, Dillard, March 21, 1961)

All else equal, unarmed disputants were likely to back down from violence when their opponent issued a weapon threat. When the unarmed party had greater strength in terms of numbers, however, submission to the armed party was likely only if the particular weapon involved was a firearm (see also Brown, February 23, 1961, in "setting").

Similar to disputes in which only one party was armed, disputes in which both parties were armed frequently resulted in violence. The main reason for this finding is that these types of disputes were most likely to emerge between rival gang members or other individuals with a preexisting hostility. Typically, one party would brandish and sometimes use a weapon to preempt or defend against a weapon attack by the opposing party. Even when both parties were armed, however, disputes did not always escalate into violence (Possession = 29.2%; Threat = 39.0%).

Mediation was the most obvious factor leading to a non-violent outcome in these disputes. When detached workers and/or other third parties took steps to prevent violence, they generally were successful at counteracting the amplificatory effect of weapons, regardless of the relationship between the offender and the victim.

Non-violent outcomes also were likely when one party of the dispute submitted to or withdrew from the other.[49] Disputants generally backed down when they were inferior in terms of weapon lethality, whether real or perceived. The following incident, excerpted from a report made by the detached worker for the Junior Imperials, illustrates this general process:

---

[49] Although there was no supporting evidence, it seems reasonable to conclude that submission by one armed party to another equally armed party would be likely to occur when the latter had a numerical advantage over the former.

Jim Morita and I went over to Ernest's [Vice Lords] house and talked to him. This was after their dance had been raided. Jim and I both talked to Ernest about the situation and about setting up a meeting with their officers. He was supposed to bring four of his officers, I was supposed to bring two of mine, and Jim was going to bring two of his. I did that in order to give him the feeling that he wasn't going to be outnumbered, so he said they'd meet us at 7:30 at Sears Y. I was a little late in getting there last night. I got over to Larry's house at about 7:20 and, thinking that five minutes at Sears wouldn't make any difference, we instead watched a TV program. Then, we picked up Bo, Ivory, and Lester [Junior Imperials] and went back to the Y. Well, when they were going up the stairs, they saw Ernest and about four of his boys coming down the stairs. I didn't see them, but they tell me when I got in there that the meeting was over. I thought they were joking, but Jim confirmed it, saying that Ernest and his boys had been there, and one of Jim's boys, a boy named Johnny [Midget Imperial Chaplains], had brought a .32 automatic with him, and they claimed that Ernest and three of his boys had weapons. One of them had a stick and another a knife. They had passed words and Ernest had threatened Johnny, claiming he's going to get all of their officers, and Johnny said, "Come on, mother fucker (inaudible). I'm prepared." And, they claimed that Ernest's guys only had zip guns, and Johnny had an automatic. A zip gun will only shoot once and without accuracy, and they figured that Johnny had the edge on them because of the automatic. So, Ernest said, "Well, there's no need for a meeting, because your boy got a gun," so Jim said, "Well, give me the gun, Johnny." Ernest and his boys kicked their chairs over and walked out. There were two knives and a gun, and that one was Johnny's, and it only had one bullet. (Detached Worker Report, Mitchell, September 29, 1959)

The observer who had actually witnessed the incident offered the following information:

Jim drove to 15th and Holman, where there were about a dozen fellows standing on the porch of a building. He told the fellows that only the war counselor, president, and vice-president would be taken to the meeting. Lobo and Jackie got into the car. He then asked the fellows where was Kilroy, the war counselor of the Midgets. They told him that he had gone home. We saw Lester standing on a corner a block away, and Jim called him over to the car to ask him where he thought his fellow lived. Lester got into the car and took us to the house of the boy. Kilroy got into the car and we drove to the Sears YMCA. There were two tables in the [Maple] room placed end to end. There were only eight chairs in the room, and Jim remarked that this was not enough chairs. Just as Jim said this, Ernest, Bobby [their elected vice-president], and two unnamed young men walked up to the room and came in. The Imperials that were in the room were seated all around the table instead of on one side. The Vice Lords came in and stood around the walls, behind the chairs of those Imperials that were seated. I went into the next room and started to drag some chairs into the room. When I re-entered the room, Ernest was making a sort of clicking sound with his tongue and waving his thumb and forefinger, which was in the form of a bulls-eye, at each of the fellows. This was as if to say, "I have you in my sights." Jim had left the room and had not returned. Several of the Imperials asked Ernest what he meant by all those actions, and he told Lester that he had until 10:00 P.M. to live. So, the room became filled with invectives and counter threats. After a few minutes, Jim returned with some chairs. He started to tell the fellows that they should try to change their attitude about each other before the meeting, thereby allowing the meeting to produce something positive from them. Ernest then got up and told Jim that he did not think that someone should always warn them, because they usually were not the ones who start the trouble. Jim told them all to be quiet. Johnny told them that they should listen to Jim. Ernest again said that he thought it was wrong of them [the workers] to always be talking to him when he knew that his boys did not always start the trouble. At this point, Ernest got up out of the chair that he was sitting in and came over to the chair that Johnny was sitting in and asked Johnny if he had a gun ["heat"]. Johnny told him no. Ernest then said that he was a liar and that if Jim really meant all this talk about let's have some peace he should at least make sure that he and his could come to a meeting without being under the threat of the guns of the Imperials. Jim then went over to Johnny and asked him if he had any heat. Johnny told him no. Ernest called Johnny a liar and said that if Johnny did not give Jim the heat there would be no meeting. Jim again asked Johnny if he had any heat and Johnny forthwith produced a .32 caliber automatic. Ernest immediately shrieked that there would be no meeting, since the Imperials could not be trusted. He then told his boys "let's go." They left and Jim then asked the fellows if any other fellow had heat. Soo Baby pulled out a knife and gave it to Jim. Just then, Ed Mitchell came in the room with the Juniors and the Seniors. (Observer Report, Wright, September 28, 1959)

The next excerpt, reported by the detached worker with the Vampires, contains another incident in which a non-violent outcome was induced by a (perceived) disparity in weapon lethality:

When I was leaving [the parade on Friday night], I saw a group of fellows gathering, and they had baseball bats and sticks and stuff like that and they were debating whether they should fight this other group there and one boy said, "Man, we had better leave them alone, because I know they got their heats with them and bats and sticks aren't going to help us, so we had better leave them alone." I don't know who they were referring to, but all the fights that were supposed to come off between the Lords and the Cobras didn't. (Detached Worker Report, Mitchell, August 16, 1960)

Even though Ernest and his boys (in the first incident) and the group of fellows that the Vampires' worker saw gathering as he was leaving (in the second incident) were both armed, each backed down from a potentially violent confrontation. In cases such as these, submission or withdrawal by one party clearly was influenced by a disparity in weapon lethality.

Overall, then, these data begin to lay bare the complexities underlying the finding based on quantitative data of a tendency for disputes to escalate into violence with the introduction of weaponry by only one party or by both parties. Much of the violence in disputes involving an armed party against an unarmed party took the form of a surprise attack stemming from preexisting hostilities, usually between members of rival gangs. In the remaining cases, the unarmed party appeared more prone to attack the armed party than vice versa. Circumstances favorable to this outcome were those that either prevented perception of or nullified the risks associated with violence against an armed opponent. Disputes involving weaponry on both sides were even more likely to be resolved violently, mainly because they typically emerged between rival gang members or other individuals with preexisting hostility. With rare exception (e.g., some disputes between entire gangs), however, violence was avoided in these and most other disputes involving weapons, either on only one or both sides, when a detached worker and/or third party mediated or when one party retreated from an opponent who held a numerical or weapons advantage. Both of these situational factors served as an indication that violence would be particularly costly and that backing down almost certainly would not result in a loss of face.

Co-offenders and Co-victims

Co-offenders and co-victims strongly impacted the way in which dispute-related incidents unfolded. Quantitative data show that both the presence and behavior of co-offenders and co-victims were important predictors of dispute outcome. As demonstrated here, their relative numbers, including how an approximate balance or imbalance interacted with other situational factors, also were influential.

Disputes involving approximately equal numbers of co-offenders and co-victims tended to escalate into violence, especially if there was preexisting hostility between disputants and/or agitation. All else equal, disputants in these circumstances were expected to behave violently and were rewarded with status if they performed well. To back down was to lose face. The complexities of situational contexts, however, meant that all else frequently was not equal. Depending on the operation of other factors, violence could be and often was avoided.

Although non-violent outcomes were most likely when a detached worker and/or some other third party mediated, violence was sometimes squashed when one party of the dispute submitted or showed deference to the other either because of the latter's threatened use of weaponry or out of respect for the latter's position of authority or influence within the gang context. The incident reported in the following excerpt is an example of how submission from one party could be elicited by a weapon threat issued by the other:

> Henry quit school. And, the next day he went over to Crane...him and Buck. A couple of guys [Braves] saw them...(inaudible) saw Henry and Buck and said, "You guys are Cobras, aren't you?" Buck and Henry stopped and said, "Yeah, we are Cobras." They said, "Well, we are going to kick your ass." So, Henry put his hand in his pocket (inaudible) and Buck put his hand against (inaudible) "an ass kicking isn't worth being killed over," and "Yeah, we are just playing. We can get you guys later." So, they left. That happened Monday. (Detached Worker Report, Dryden, October 27, 1960)

Notwithstanding the relatively equal number of participants on each side of this dispute, violence was avoided when members of the Braves withdrew after apparent weapon threats by Henry and Buck of the Egyptian Cobras. As with mediation and deference based on the offender-victim relationship, unequal armament—real or perceived—not only signaled to the relevant party that violence under the current conditions would be costly but that there also was a face-saving reason for backing down.

Disputes involving severe imbalance in numbers of co-offenders and co-victims were also likely to be resolved non-violently, with the outnumbered party submitting or withdrawing. An apposite case is an incident in which five Vice Lords decide not to jack up one of the Midget Imperial Chaplains as soon as he receives backup from 20 other Midgets who happened to be on the scene:

> [Lobo] related an incident to the effect that they [the Vice Lords] had come up to his house and threatened Johnny. He lives a little bit out of the area. And, the Vice Lords came there, and about five of them were going to jack Johnny up. They didn't realize that there were 20 other Midgets on the porch when they came into the area. And, when they started, when it seemed they were coming to blows, the Midgets came to Johnny's aid, and the Vice Lords took off. (Detached Worker Report, Mitchell, September 29, 1959)

The worker for the South Side Cobras reported briefly on a similar incident involving some unknown group and the Cobras:

> They spent Christmas at a dance at The Pershing. Everybody got tore up and went to The Pershing to the dance. They said some group I don't know was going to jack up the Cobras—Michael and Happy and Chucky—but when they got downstairs there were about 35 Cobras, so they decided not to do it. (Detached Worker Report, Ross, January 5, 1961)

Reporting on what he had been told by some of the gang boys he sponsored, the detached worker with the Stateway Cobras relates another incident in which the unequal number of participants on each side appeared to be critical in bringing about a non-violent resolution:

> [Last night] we were en route to the Duncan YMCA for a ball game, and this subject came up of strip-poker and how they played up at this girl's home. And, there seems to be a little animosity developing between Bear, who's the president of the club, and some of the other boys in the club, namely, Ralph, Bernard, and Marvin, because Bear used to go with this girl and still is going with her, and he walked in up there last

week, and they said it was about 2:30 or 3:00 in the afternoon, and they were right in the middle of a strip-poker game. The girl didn't have on anything but a bra. And, Tojo had on a sport coat, a shirt, and a tie, and that's all he had on. And so, when Bear walked in, he didn't know this had been going on up there and he wanted to know what's happening. He asked, "What you guys doing up here?" That's supposed to be his girlfriend. Well, he didn't like it all, so Ralph tried to get him to get in the game. Bear was real belligerent. In fact, he let them know he didn't go for that at all. They had this strip-poker game going when Bear got there and Bear took the girl in the back. They don't know what happened when he took her in the back. But, he was pissed off because he caught her in that way. Well, there were too many of them for him to fight them all, so he took the girl in the back. Well, that broke up the strip-poker game. (Detached Worker Report, Smith, January 15, 1960)

The next excerpt, reported by one of the observers, contains an incident in which an unequal number of participants again seems to contribute to the development of a non-violent outcome:

Vince [Dukes] did most of the talking on the way out to John's house. For the most part, he talked of different fights he had been in from time to time. The longest incident he related concerned a misunderstanding between himself and a guy he had seen just briefly three times in his whole life. The guy came up to him and told him to "stay away from my girl." Vince did not even know what girl he was talking about, but his brother who was present said, "Let's get a bat and clobber this guy." Vince and his brother then went out looking for this guy and found him. At the time, Vince had many of his friends with him, and he told the guy he wanted to straighten things out. But, Vince realized that the guy could not say much with all of Vince's friends there, so Vince told him, "Look, I know you can't say anything, because I got too many friends here. I'll tell you what. I'll meet you tomorrow, and if you still feel the same way, we battle it out, just the two of us." With that, he left. He saw the guy the next day, and they discussed the situation. In doing so, Vince said, they found out they had no real quarrel. (Observer Report, Pope, September 20, 1959)

These incidents reveal a tendency for disputants to back down from violent confrontation with a numerically superior opponent. In the first three incidents, the potential offender is reportedly motivated to engage in violence but, upon realizing the numerical advantage possessed by the victim, withdraws entirely from the encounter. In the last incident, the victim is badly outnumbered by his opponent (Vince of the Dukes) and therefore puts forth no resistance. In turn, his opponent offers him a face-saving way out of the dispute, saying "Look, I know you can't say anything, because I got too many friends here. I'll tell you what. I'll meet you tomorrow, and if you still feel the same way, we battle it out, just the two of us." This suggests a general recognition of the importance of numbers and the acceptability of backing down from violence when at a numerical disadvantage.

Non-violent resolutions to these types of disputes came less easily when preexisting hostilities (e.g., inter-gang rivalry, retaliation, etc.) and/or intoxicants were involved. In cases involving preexisting hostility, a group of individuals simply would attack, usually without warning, a smaller number of individuals who they held in contempt or who were in some way associated with the real target of their hostility. Perhaps because intoxicants impair recognition of costs and contribute to a discounting of them, those under the influence did not always back down, even when faced with a severe numerical disadvantage.

Overall, these data show that, in addition to the presence and behavior of co-offenders and co-victims, it was necessary to consider their relative numbers as well as the operation of other situational contingencies. Unless circumstances suggested to one of the parties that violence would be costly but that backing down would not be or at least would be much less so, disputes in which there was a relative balance in the number of co-offenders and co-victims could be expected to result in violence, especially when the rewards of such behavior were enhanced by preexisting hostility between the disputants and/or instigation. In contrast, an imbalance in the number of co-offenders and co-victims more frequently led to non-violent dispute outcomes. The unfair advantage held by the numerically superior party appeared not only to increase the risk of violence for the other (outnumbered) party but also to provide the latter with an opportunity to back down without suffering a consequential loss of face. Under these circumstances, submission or withdrawal by the outnumbered party was considered to be acceptable behavior and, as suggested by the astonishment and admiration expressed by individuals who witnessed others standing up to a numerically superior opponent (even if they lost), was generally expected as well. However, because of their adverse effect on the rational decision-making process, intoxicants and preexisting hostilities both tended to mitigate against the impact of unequal numbers.

CHAPTER 8

DISCUSSION AND CONCLUSION

KEY FINDINGS

Criminology traditionally has neglected the microsocial level of explanation, and the study of violence has been hampered by an almost complete failure to appreciate the importance of understanding why potentially violent encounters sometimes are resolved non-violently. The purpose of this study was to address these two deficiencies by examining the role of various situational characteristics and interaction processes in the development and (violent or non-violent) resolution of dispute-related incidents within the social context of adolescent street gangs. Toward this end, data from detached worker and observer reports on 12 black and 8 white gangs in Chicago during the late 1950s and early 1960s were analyzed (with dispute-related incidents as the unit of analysis). While quantitative analyses were brought to bear on hypotheses derived from impression management theory, qualitative analyses were undertaken to uncover themes related to the independent and joint influence of microsocial factors and processes.

Quantitative

Quantitative analyses involved testing hypotheses derived from impression management theory, each focused on assessing the importance of one of several situational variables suggested by the literature as relevant to an adequate conceptualization of violence— setting, offender-victim relationship, victim behavior, third parties, intoxicants, weaponry, and co-offenders and co-victims. When possible, interaction sequences also were examined. Results generally are supportive.

Dispute-related incidents emerged most often: (1) in public settings in which both the offender and victim typically hung out, (2) as a result of a social control process initiated by a norm- or order-violation on the part of the victim, (3) between a gang member and an individual with no known gang affiliation (though with whom the gang boy was likely to be in close contact), and (4) in front of an external audience. However, impression management theory suggests that dispute outcome cannot be determined solely on the basis of frequency of occurrence. Whether disputes escalate into violence or are squashed depends, instead, on the extent to which circumstances indicate to disputants that, in terms of their situated identity, one outcome is more favorable than the other. Thus, on one hand, the likelihood of disputes escalating into violence can be expected to increase when the potential status rewards of such behavior are especially high, as are the status costs of doing otherwise. Non-violent dispute outcomes, on the other hand, should be more likely when violence has no bearing on status or is less socially acceptable than backing down. For the most part, both of these predictions were supported by the data. Findings clearly show violence to have developed most often in high-stakes character contests, such as those involving a territorial component, those between members of rival gangs, those in which the external audience instigated, and those in which both parties were armed. Perhaps because of their adverse effect on disputants' perception and definition of the situation, intoxicants also increased the likelihood of violence. Conversely, when victim acquiescence made it unnecessary for the offender to resort to violence in order to maintain status or when members of the external audience made clear their disapproval of violence (and thus approval of retreat), non-violent resolutions more often were reached.

Although these findings are consistent with theoretical expectations, contrary findings also emerged. Neither victim resistance nor the presence of bystanders who were predicted to be most apt to approve of violence (i.e., male youth) increased the likelihood of a violent dispute outcome. Moreover, neither the possession nor threatened use of weaponry by only one party significantly reduced violence; in fact, both were associated with a lower, not higher, likelihood of a non-violent dispute outcome. Taken as a whole, however, the evidence reported in this study is supportive of the theory, indicating that disputes generally unfolded in a manner consistent with what we would expect given the circumstances and their impression (status) management implications.

Qualitative
Qualitative analyses provide greater insight into the specific conditions under which disputes escalated into violence or were resolved non-violently. In general, results indicate that the unfolding of disputes was influenced to a large extent by the interrelated effects of situational factors and processes, particularly status management, on disputants' subjective assessment of the utility and risk of violence vis-à-vis that of retreat.

Disputes were most likely to escalate into violence when situational cues suggested to disputants that violent behavior not only represented a means by which to enhance status (and sometimes exact revenge) but was necessary for the maintenance of it. This is why violent outcomes were characteristic of disputes in which territorial rights were at stake, members of rival gangs were involved, the external audience and/or co-offenders or co-victims engaged in instigating behavior, both parties were armed, or the victim challenged the offender (frequently because of the influence of intoxicants). In all cases, heightened status concerns meant that violence was especially valued and that backing down almost certainly would result in a loss of face.

To understand why disputes, including the high-stakes ones mentioned above, often were resolved non-violently, it is important to consider the operation of a number of factors that mitigated against the use of violence. Despite the fact that their impact occasionally was counteracted by preexisting hostility (sometimes manifested in a surprise weapon or non-weapon attack) and intoxicants, both of which tended to impede behavior that would qualify as rational given the circumstances, situational cues that contributed to non-violent dispute outcomes were, for the most part, alike in suggesting to disputants that violence was potentially more costly than backing down. The one exception was victim acquiescence, which served as an indication to the offender that violence simply was not needed in order to maintain face.

First, intervention by members of the external audience proved critical to the development of many non-violent dispute outcomes. When detached workers and/or other third parties intervened (protected/mediated), the clear message sent to the target(s) of their effort was that they were unfavorable toward violence and that backing down was more socially acceptable. Detached workers engaged in such behavior for a variety of reasons, e.g., when a dispute placed the use of a valued facility at risk; when disputes occurred within the gang with which they were working or between members of friendly gangs; and/or when disputes appeared to be potentially very serious, as when weapons were involved or when neither party seemed willing to back down (frequently because of the influence of intoxicants). Their tendency to mediate under these circumstances at least partly explains why male youth bystanders (who were likely to be present during intra-gang and friendly inter-gang disputes) and victim resistance (which would signal to onlookers that serious consequences might be forthcoming if nothing was done to stop the dispute) both were shown to be statistically related to non-violent dispute outcomes. After detached workers, male youth were most likely to act as mediating third parties, particularly when disputes involved intra-gang members, members of two friendly gangs, or their detached worker.

Although not as explicit, the presence of bystanding detached workers or other authority figures suggested much the same to disputants as did direct intervention, i.e., violence would be met with disapproval, whereas retreat would not. The regular presence of detached workers during disputes with bystanding male youth was suggested as another reason that these types of disputes were statistically more likely to be resolved non-violently than were disputes initiated in the presence of other types of bystanders.

In addition to the behavior and characteristics of the external audience, both the situated identity of disputants and their relationship to one another had important implications. Disputes were likely to be resolved non-violently when one party was up against an opponent who was in some way socially inadequate (e.g., extremely intoxicated, small, physically disabled, etc.), an opponent who was of greater influence within the gang context, or an opponent who was in a position of authority. Violence with any of these people, even if they were resistant, generally was disapproved, and those who did not withdraw from confrontations with them clearly were risking loss of face.

Disputes also tended to be resolved non-violently when one party backed down from an opponent who possessed a fearsome reputation, demonstrated an overwhelming readiness to fight, or held a numerical and/or weapon advantage. Even though violence done well under these circumstances could result in status enhancement, the odds clearly were not favorable and suggested instead that physical harm, most likely accompanied by a loss of face, would be forthcoming. In contrast, retreat placed only status at risk or, when outnumbered or out-armed, was considered to be socially acceptable. Retreat, then, would not necessarily be met with more approval than violence, but it certainly was perceived by the relevant party as potentially much less costly.

Finally, victim acquiescence often was sufficient for the development of a non-violent dispute outcome. By counteracting the altercasting effect of previous resistance or by preventing the occurrence of altercasting altogether, conciliatory measures appeared to alleviate the pressure on the offender to maintain face through the use of violence. As with mediation, the fact that victims oftentimes took conciliatory measures only after initial resistance (and verbal sanctioning by the offender) helps explain the unexpected negative relationship observed between victim resistance and dispute outcome.

Together, qualitative findings show how the decision made by disputants to enter into violence or to back down tended to reflect the combined impact of various situational factors on their assessment of the utility and risk of each behavior. Status (i.e., impression management) considerations clearly were central to this process. Individuals within the gang context experienced a great deal of pressure to manage their status—both individual and gang—through violent behavior (or a willingness for it), and those who backed down without a legitimate reason were likely to suffer a loss of face. While in many cases fear surely underlay the desire to back down, it did not qualify as a legitimate reason in this social milieu. Thus, individuals were most apt to back down when circumstances suggested that they could do so without appearing to be afraid or that they had to do so in order to maintain a favorable situated identity (e.g., if a third party intervened or otherwise conveyed an expectation for such behavior, if the opposing party acquiesced or possessed a poor situated identity, or if the offender-victim relationship warranted submission/withdrawal). Backing down also was permissible when fear clearly was justifiable and honor was not compromised (e.g., if faced with an unfair numerical or weapons disadvantage). If none of these options were available, individuals could have been expected to engage in violence, unless the physical and social costs of doing so were perceived to outweigh the social costs of backing down (e.g., when one's opponent possessed a fearsome reputation and/or displayed an overwhelming readiness to engage in violence). The specific operation of this process was contingent on the absence of intoxicants, however, since their consumption frequently was shown to have had an adverse effect on the ability of disputants to act rationally.

LIMITATIONS

Despite the strength of these findings, several limitations of this research need to be mentioned. Aside from the missing data problem, which was discussed earlier (see Chapter 5) and will not be detailed further here, one limitation is the potential unreliability of the data in terms of both source (who) and quality (what). In approximately three-quarters of the ("serious") cases that were analyzed (2490 or 78%), the source of information was discernable. Of these, well over half (72%) were based on direct observation. The remaining 696 cases involved the detached workers or observers reporting on what they had been told either by actual participants (22.5%), non-participant observers (4.2%), or non-participant non-observers (1.2%). Obviously, the use of secondhand information is problematic. Such cases, however, did not weigh heavily into the analysis because of their relatively small numbers and the limited amount of useful material they typically contained. Perhaps of greater significance, then, is the variation in the quality of reports based on direct observation. Because detached workers were interviewed at weekly or bi-weekly intervals, they were not always able to recall comprehensively and/or accurately the dispute-related incidents they had observed. In addition, despite the fact that "the research team actively discouraged workers from imputing theoretical significance to what they observed" (Short 2002), the perception of some of the detached workers and what they eventually reported may have been influenced by ideas about the importance of such things as status threats and Cloward and Ohlin's (1960) opportunity structure, to which they had been exposed in staff meetings and in interaction with members of the research team. The reliability of some of the detached worker reports also may have been compromised by intentional distortion. While detached workers were informed of the strict rules of confidentiality adhered to by the research team,[50] they were aware that the information contained within their reports would be read by members of the research team who were held in high regard and were known to be closely associated with the Director of the Program for Detached Workers. Thus, certain workers occasionally may have exaggerated the role they played in preventing disputes from escalating into violence or may have downplayed their own instigative behaviors or the amount and seriousness of violence that occurred in their presence. Some of the workers also may have misrepresented the truth in order to provide the interviewer (and those higher up in the research organization) with information that they believed was desired.

Although potential unreliability appears to be especially serious concerning the data where reasons for behaviors are coded, a number of strategies were adopted to prevent the data from being compromised. Throughout the research, pains were taken to minimize the use of imputations. Further, reports from multiple workers were combined when possible, with each acting as a check against the other. Information provided by the observers also offset problems associated with the detached worker reports. While observers accompanied only some of the detached workers, and did so on a periodic basis, their reports were more detailed than the detached worker reports and were less susceptible to problems with recall, as their reports typically were made within a day or two after the most recent period of observation.

---

[50] In particular, they were assured that program administrators would not have access to the worker reports.

Another limitation is the potential problem with reliability of the coding. As in all research involving interpretation, researcher bias and errors may limit the adequacy of the data and the results. However, analysis of interrater agreement indicates that, in this research, unreliability of the data does not constitute a significant problem.

Finally, the generalizability of findings is limited. Because the data consist of disputes occurring within the social milieu of adolescent street gangs operating in inner-city Chicago neighborhoods during the late 1950s and early 1960s, it is inappropriate to conclude that situational factors and interaction processes necessarily will have similar effects beyond this particular context. Nevertheless, consistent findings from studies based on entirely different types of samples (e.g., Luckenbill 1977 and Felson 1982, 1984) suggests the findings reported here may transcend both time and place.

Limitations notwithstanding, ethnographic data are ideal in that they afford researchers unique opportunities to examine from close proximity the dynamic processes of ongoing interaction. Thus, ethnographic studies designed specifically for the purpose of analyzing the influence of the microsocial level in dispute-related incidents (and other behaviors of interest to criminologists) occurring both within and outside the gang context would make especially valuable contributions. Positive contributions also would be made by future research involving comparative analyses of these Chicago gang data and data on disputes that occur in more contemporary settings, as this would permit assessment of the extent to which the importance of the microsocial level varies across time and place.

IMPLICATIONS

The implications of this research are twofold: basic and applied. Findings provide some indication of the benefit to be had in the study of violence by focusing more attention on the microsocial level and by adopting a comparative framework. Because situational factors and interaction processes were shown to affect both the occurrence and outcome of potentially violent disputes, significant advances in understanding violence are likely to accrue only if the microsocial level receives more scholarly consideration and is integrated with individual- and macro-levels of explanation. Of course, precision of this understanding ultimately depends on adequate conceptualization, with violence being recognized as one of several possible outcomes.

Impression management theory is suggested as a unifying framework from which to approach the analysis of microsocial phenomena in the development of both violent and non-violent disputes. Early statements, which drew from Goffman's (1955, 1959, 1967) classic work on social interaction, emphasized the face-saving property of violent behavior; that is, violence was seen as the result of a rational decision-making process in which the perpetrator perceives the maintenance of an acceptable social identity to be contingent on the use force. These statements echoed ideas previously encompassed by the status threat hypothesis, as advanced by Short and Strodtbeck (1965). The status threat hypothesis suggests that the decision made by gang boys, particularly gang leaders, to participate in violence (as opposed to remain aloof) is the outcome of a subjective utility-risk calculation in which the potential gains and losses of status within the immediate context of the gang are weighed against the more remote possibility of punitive responses from the larger society. Richard Felson and his colleagues (e.g., Felson 1978, 1981, 1984; Felson and Steadman 1983) provided further impetus to impression management theory, highlighting theoretically and empirically the importance of violence as a means of saving face. In addition, they identified a number of conditions associated with non-violent resolutions of potentially violent encounters, such as backing down because the costs are perceived as too high, because of the poor situated identity or acquiescent behavior of one of the antagonists, or because of mediating third parties. The current research builds on these previous efforts by demonstrating the usefulness of impression management theory as a conceptual scheme from which to understand and explain how various situational factors operate (independently and in combination) within the gang context to produce either violent or non-violent dispute outcomes.

It must be noted, however, that impression management theory is limited in two ways not identified previously. First, there is lack of clarity regarding the relative importance of gaining status as opposed to not losing it. The primacy of the latter is implied by an almost exclusive focus on efforts undertaken to "save," "protect," and "recover" face. Pursuit of status has not been given much consideration, except in relation and response to potential status threats or losses. The theoretical interpretation advocated here differs in that it explicitly recognizes unprovoked attempts to gain status but is similar in viewing the concern for not losing status as being more central to overall impression management. Individuals within the gang context clearly wished to look good and actively sought—if they did not create—opportunities to demonstrate to observers their bravery and concomitant claim to recognition, especially against members rival gangs. However, deliberate testing and challenging of others in order to gain status occurred primarily when situational cues suggested that the risk of losing face was low, e.g., because the possession of a numerical or weapons advantage minimized the chance that these others would be willing to fight back or actually do much damage if they did. Enthusiasm for confrontation generally was not as apparent in cases involving greater potential for looking bad. Yet, before backing down from any type of challenge, disputants first had to take into account the possibility that such behavior would result in a loss of status and, if so, how the loss compared to the potential costs of doing battle. If the costs of backing down outweighed the costs of violence, disputes were likely to escalate. Gang boys (and others) thus engaged in violent behavior in large part because they felt they had to, not necessarily because they wanted to. Retreat could be expected mainly when status was not jeopardized or when the risk to status appeared to be outweighed by the negative consequences associated with violence, which could be social only or both social and physical. Within the social milieu of gang boys, then, concern appeared to be focused primarily on not looking bad and secondarily on looking good. More information is needed to understand how differences between individuals (both in gang and other social contexts) influence the operation of both of these important components of impression management.

The other, related problem with impression management theory is its inability to explain contrary cases—(1) potentially violent encounters that are status threatening to disputants but nevertheless are resolved non-violently and (2) potentially violent encounters that escalate into actual violence despite the potential for great physical and/or social costs and the availability of a socially acceptable reason for at least one of the parties to back down. Although intoxicants and preexisting hostilities have been identified as contingencies that affect the operation of the central causal process, surely there are additional factors that impinge on interaction sequences and the (rational) decisions that actors make as they weigh status concerns against the alternatives at each point along the way.

Elijah Anderson's "staging area" concept may help to explain why violence occurs even when, on the basis of impression management theory, we might not expect it. According to Anderson (1999:77):

> People from other neighborhoods who come to a staging area and present themselves are said to be "representing" both who they are and the "world" or " 'hood" from which they hail. To represent is to place one's area of the city on the line, to say to outsiders, "Hey, this is what's to me [what I am made of] and my neighborhood," compared with other neighborhoods of the city. For the boldest young people, it is to put oneself on the line, in effect, to put a chip on one's shoulder and dare others to knock it off. It is to wage a campaign for respect, but with the added elements of dare and challenge. There are often enough young people in the staging area to provide the critical mass of negative energy necessary to spark violence, not just against people like themselves but also against others present in the staging area, creating a flashpoint for violence.

In staging areas, the pressure to maintain status is extraordinarily intense, and the point of no return may be reached much more rapidly in these contexts than in others. Anderson (1999:79) states, "As the situation deteriorates, it may be very difficult for either party to back down, particularly if members of an audience are present who have, or are understood to have, a significant social investment in who and what each participant pretends to be." Under these types of circumstances (which were most likely in rival gang disputes), Chicago gang boys sometimes gambled against the odds and entered into battle despite the presence of a face-saving reason for retreat, such as a numerical or weapons disadvantage. The status payoff typically was great, even in defeat.

Although the staging area notion is useful, it leaves unanswered the question of why some people did not succumb to the intensity of these situations. That is, why did some gang boys choose flight over fight in rival gang conflicts, eschewing the "campaign for respect" and group norms in favor of violence and against peer abandonment? Individual level differences between gang boys certainly are part of the explanation (see Cartwright et al. 1980 for discussion of measured within-gang personality variations). Short of much more complete knowledge about each individual and the interactions between them, an adequate accounting of the relative import of each is not likely. Perhaps a promising line of inquiry would begin with an assessment of the extent to which variations in interpretations and reactions to situational cues (or "provocations") are influenced by differing control ratios among individuals (see Tittle 1995).

On occasion, individual level factors obviously had a greater impact on the unfolding of disputes than did situational ones. While violence in these cases appeared to be brought about mainly by "craziness" and fatalistic attitudes that developed out of frequent trouble with the law and/or a continuous cycle of retaliatory attacks, some evidence pointed toward the influence of limited cognitive abilities (e.g., perception and/or reasoning). The occurrence of such anomalies further suggests the need to integrate levels of explanation.

Incorporating individual level factors into impression management theory also may enhance its ability to explain those cases in which gang boys elected not to fight even at the risk of losing face. This research identified potential physical and social costs that prevented violence with an opponent who possessed a fearsome reputation or who otherwise appeared capable of inflicting serious harm, but in a few cases disputes were resolved non-violently despite the absence of these situational considerations. Some gang boys simply would not fight because of their lack of ability, recently acquired stake in conformity, and/or fear of formal or informal sanctions. Oftentimes, these boys were fringe members for whom status in the gang world was unrealistic or relatively unimportant.

Clearly, more work on impression management theory is needed. A solid foundation has now been laid, but much remains to be done. Before significant advances can be made in our understanding of violence and thus before effective preventative policies can be devised, it is imperative that theoretical limitations be addressed. Efforts to integrate impression management theory with macro and individual level explanations will make especially valuable contributions.

In the meantime, perhaps one policy implication of the current research is that developing and actively promoting sources of status other than violence among youth—especially within the gang milieu—should be encouraged, as violent behavior has been found to be a means by which to look good and especially to avoid looking bad in the presence of others. In addition, evidence showing the effectiveness of detached workers in reducing violence among Chicago gangs in the late 1950s and early 1960s suggests that a "nothing works" approach is untenable.[51] Implementation of a detached worker program may be a promising solution to the gang problem in modern society (cf. Klein 1971). However, a key lesson learned from the detached worker program in Chicago is that more effective strategies are needed to deal with the fluid nature of the gang world and the concomitant challenge of keeping gangs and individual members under constant supervision.

---

[51] Unfortunately, official data that would allow for comparisons of rates of violence before and after the detached worker program are not available.

References

Amir, Menachem. 1971. *Patterns in Forcible Rape*. Chicago: University of Chicago Press.

Anderson, Elijah. 1990. *Streetwise; Race, Class, and Change in an Urban Community*. Chicago: University of Chicago Press.

_____. 1998. "The Social Ecology of Youth Violence." Pp. 65-104 in *Crime and Justice: A Review of Research*, edited by Michael Tonry and Mark H. Moore v. 24. Chicago: University of Chicago Press.

_____. 1999. *Code of the Streets: Decency, violence, and the moral life of the inner city*. New York: W.W. Norton and Company.

Argyle, Michael, Adrian Furnham, and Jean Ann Graham. 1981. *Social Situations*. Cambridge, UK: Cambridge University Press.

Athens, Lonnie H. 1977. "Violent Crime: A Symbolic Interactionist Study." *Symbolic Interaction* 1:56-70.

Athens, Lonnie H. 1980. *Violent Criminal Acts and Actors*. London: Routledge.

Ball-Rokeach, Sandra J. 1973. "Values and Violence: A Test of the Subculture of Violence Thesis." *American Sociological Review* 38:736-49.

Banitt, Rivka, Shoshana Katznelson, and Shlomit Streit. 1970. "The Situational Aspects of Violence: A Research Model." Pp. 241-58 in *Israel Studies in Criminology*, edited by Shlomo Shoham. Tel-Aviv, Israel: Gomeh Publishing House.

Battin, Sara R., Karl G. Hill, Robert D. Abbott, Richard F. Catalano, and J. David Hawkins. 1998. "The Contribution of Gang Membership to Delinquency beyond Delinquent Friends." *Criminology* 36(1):93-115.

Baumer, Eric, Julie Horney, Richard Felson, and Janet L. Lauritsen. 2003. "Neighborhood Disadvantage and the Nature of Violence." *Criminology* 41(1):39-72.

Berdie, Ralph F. 1947. "Playing the Dozens." *Journal of Abnormal and Social Psychology* 42:120-21.

Berkowitz, Leonard. 1978. "Is Criminal Violence Normative Behavior? Hostile and Instrumental Aggression in Violent Incidents." *Journal of Research in Crime and Delinquency* 15:148-61.

_____. 1986. "Some Varieties on Human Aggression: Criminal Violence as Coercion, Rule-Following, Impression Management and Impulsive Behavior." Pp. 87-103 in *Violent Transactions: The Limits of Personality*, edited by Anne Campbell and John J. Gibbs. Oxford: Basil Blackwell.

Berkowitz, Leonard and Anthony LePage. 1967. "Weapons as Aggression-Eliciting Stimuli." *Journal of Personality and Social Psychology* 7(2):202-07.

Birbeck, Christopher and Gary LaFree. 1993. "The Situational Analysis of Crime and Deviance." *Annual Review of Sociology* 19:113-37.

Black, Donald. 1983. "Crime as Social Control." *American Sociological Review* 48:34-45.

Block, Richard. 1977. *Violent Crime: Environment, Interaction, and Death.* Lexington, MA: Lexington Books.

_____. 1981. "Victim-Offender Dynamics in Violent Crime." *Journal of Criminal Law and Criminology* 72(2):743-61.

Block, Richard and Westley G. Skogan. 1986. "Resistance and Nonfatal Outcomes in Stranger-to-Stranger Predatory Crime." *Violence and Victims* 1(4):241-53.

Blum, Richard H. 1981. "Violence, Alcohol, and Setting: An Unexplored Nexus." Pp. 110-42 in *Drinking and Crime: Perspectives on the Relationship between Alcohol Consumption and Criminal Behavior*, edited by James J. Collins, Jr. New York: The Guilford Press.

Borden, Richard J. 1975. "Witnessed Aggression: Influence of an Observer's Sex and Values on Aggressive Responding." *Journal of Personality and Social Psychology* 31(3):567-73.

Borden, Richard J. and Stuart P. Taylor. 1973. "The Social Instigation and Control of Physical Aggression." *Journal of Applied Social Psychology* 3(4):354-61.

Borden, Richard J., Ray Bowen, and Stuart P. Taylor. 1971. "Shock Setting Behavior as a Function of Physical Attack and Extrinsic Reward." *Perceptual and Motor Skills* 33(2):563-68.

Briar, Scott and Irving Piliavin. 1965. "Delinquency, Situational Inducements, and Commitment to Conformity." *Social Problems* 13:35-45.

Brown, Bert R. 1968. "The Effects of Need to Maintaining Face on Interpersonal Bargaining." *Journal of Experimental Social Psychology* 4:107-22.

Brown, Robert C., Jr. and James T. Tedeschi. 1976. "Determinants of Perceived Aggression." *Journal of Social Psychology* 100:77-87.

Bullock, Henry Allen. 1955. "Urban Homicide in Theory and Fact." *Journal of Criminal Law and Criminology* 45:565-75.

Buss, Arnold, Ann Booker, and Edith Buss. 1972. "Firing a Weapon and Aggression." *Journal of Personality and Social Psychology* 22(3):296-302.

Campbell, Anne. 1982. "Female Aggression." Pp. 137-50 in *Aggression and Violence*, edited by Peter Marsh and Anne Campbell. New York: St. Martin's Press.

_____. 1986. "The Streets and Violence." Pp. 115-32 in *Violent Transactions: The Limits of Personality*, edited by Anne Campbell and John J. Gibbs. Oxford: Basil Blackwell.

_____. 1991. *The Girls in the Gang*. (2nd ed.). Cambridge, MA: Blackwell.

Carlson, Michael, Amy Marcus-Newhall, and Norman Miller. 1990. "Effects of Situational Aggression Cues: A Quantitative Review." *Journal of Personality and Social Psychology* 58(4):622-33.

Cartwright, Desmond S., Hershey Schwartz, and Barbara Tomson. 1975. "Status and Gang Delinquency." Pp. 57-79 in *Gang Delinquency*, edited by Desmond S. Cartwright, Barbara Tomson, and Hershey Schwartz. Monterey, CA: Brooks/Cole Publishing.

Cartwright, Desmond S., Kenneth I. Howard, and Nicholas A. Reuterman. 1970. "Multivariate Analysis of Gang Delinquency: II. Structural and Dynamic Properties of Gangs." *Multivariate Behavioral Research* 5:303-23.

_____. 1971. "Multivariate Analysis of Gang Delinquency: III. Age and Physique of Gangs and Clubs." *Multivariate Behavioral Research* 6:75-90.

_____. 1980. "Multivariate Analysis of Gang Delinquency: IV. Personality Factors in Gangs and Clubs." *Multivariate Behavioral Research* 15:3-22.

Clark, Richard D. 1995. "Lone Versus Multiple Offending in Homicide: Differences in Situational Context." *Journal of Criminal Justice* 23(5):451-60.

Cloward, Richard and Lloyd E. Ohlin. 1960. *Delinquency and Opportunity*. New York: Free Press.

Cohen, Albert K. 1955. *Delinquent Boys: The Culture of the Gang.* New York: Free Press.

_____. 1965. "The Sociology of the Deviant Act: Anomie Theory and Beyond." *American Sociological Review* 30(1):5-14.

Cohen, Albert K. and James F. Short, Jr. 1958. "Research in Delinquent Subcultures." *Journal of Social Issues* 14(3):20-37.

_____. 1976. "Crime and Juvenile Delinquency." Pp. 47-100 in *Contemporary Social Problems: An Introduction to the Sociology of Deviant Behavior and Social Organization* (4th ed.), edited by Robert K. Merton and Robert A. Nisbet. New York: Harcourt, Brace, and Jovanovich.

Cohen, Lawrence E. and Marcus Felson. 1979. "Social Change and Crime Rate Trends: A Routine Activity Approach." *American Sociological Review* 44:588-608.

Collins, James J. 1983. "Alcohol Use and Expressive Interpersonal Violence: A Proposed Explanatory Model." Pp. 5-25 in *Alcohol, Drug Abuse and Aggression*, edited by Keith A. Druley, Edward Gottheil, Thomas E. Skoloda. Springfield, IL: Charles C. Thomas.

Collins, James J., Jr. 1981. "Alcohol Use and Criminal Behavior: An Empirical, Theoretical, and Methodological Overview." Pp. 288-316 in *Drinking and Crime: Perspectives on the Relationship between Alcohol Consumption and Criminal Behavior*, edited by James J. Collins, Jr. New York: The Guilford Press.

Cook, Phillip J. 1979. "The Effect of Gun Availability on Robbery and Robbery Murder." *Policy Studies Review Annual* 3:743-81.

_____. 1981. "The Effect of Gun Availability on Violent Crime Patterns." *Annals of the American Academy of Political and Social Science* 455:63-79.

_____. 1987. "Robbery Violence." *Journal of Criminal Law and Criminology* 78(2):357-76.

Cooney, Mark. 1998. *Warriors & Peacemakers: How Third Parties Shape Violence.* New York: New York University Press.

Cornish, Derek B. and Ronald V. Clarke (Eds.). 1986. *The Reasoning Criminal.* New York: Springer-Verlag.

Coughlin, Brenda C. and Sudhir A. Venkatesh. 2003. "The Urban Street Gang after 1970." *Annual Review of Sociology* 29:41-64.

Curtis, Lynn A. 1974. "Victim Precipitation and Violent Crime." *Social Problems* 21(4):544-605.

Cusson, Maurice. 1993. "A Strategic Analysis of Crime: Criminal Tactics as Responses to Precriminal Situations." Pp. 295-304 in *Routine Activity and Rational Choice: Advances in Criminological Theory*, edited by Ronald V. Clarke and Marcus Felson. New Brunswick: Transaction Publishers.

Davidson, R.N. 1989. "Micro-Environments of Violence." Pp. 59-85 in *The Geography of Crime*, edited by David J. Evans and David T. Herbert. New York: Routledge.

Decker, Scott H. 1995. "Reconstructing Homicide Events: The Role of Witnesses in Fatal Encounters." *Journal of Criminal Justice* 23(5):439-50.
_____. 1996. "Deviant Homicide: A New Look at the Role of Motives and Victim-Offender Relationships." *Journal of Research in Crime and Delinquency* 33(4):427-49.

Denno, Deborah W. 1986. "Victim, Offender, and Situational Characteristics of Violent Crime." *Journal of Criminal Law and Criminology* 77(4):1142-58.

Epstein, Seymour and Stuart P. Taylor. 1967. "Instigation to Aggression as a Function of Defeat and Perceived Aggressive Intent of the Opponent." *Journal of Personality* 35:265-89.

Erez, Edna. 1987. "Situational or Planned Crime and the Criminal Career." Pp. 122-33 in *From Boy to Man, from Delinquency to Crime*, edited by Terence P. Thornberry Marvin E. Wolfgang, and Robert M. Figlio. Chicago: University of Chicago Press.

Erlanger, Howard S. 1979. "Estrangement, Machismo, and Gang Violence." *Social Science Quarterly* 60(2):235-48.

Esbensen, Finn-Aage and David Huizinga. 1993. "Gangs, Drugs, and Delinquency in a Survey of Urban Youth." *Criminology* 31(4):565-89.

Esbensen, Finn-Aage, Stephen Tibbetts, and Larry Gaines (Eds.). 2004. *American Youth Gangs at the Millennium*. Long Grove, IL: Waveland Press.

Fagan, Jeffrey. 1990a. "Intoxication and Aggression." Pp. 241-320 in *Crime and Justice: A Review of Research Vol. 13*, edited by Michael Tonry and James Q. Wilson. Chicago: Chicago University Press.
_____. 1990b. "Social Processes of Delinquency and Drug Use among Urban Gangs." Pp. 183-219 in *Gangs in America*, edited by C. Ronald Huff. Newbury Park, CA: Sage Publications.
_____. 1993. "Set and Setting Revisited: Influences of Alcohol and Illicit Drugs on the Social Context of Violent Events." Pp. 161-91 in *Alcohol and Interpersonal Violence: Fostering Multidisciplinary Perspectives*, edited by Susan E. Martin. Rockville, MD: U.S. Department of Health and Human Services.

Fagan, Jeffrey and Deanna L. Wilkinson. 1998. "Guns, Youth Violence, and Social Identity in Inner Cities." Pp. 105-88 in *Crime and Justice: A Review of Research*, edited by Michael Tonry and Mark H. Moore v. 24. Chicago: University of Chicago Press.

Farrington, David P. 1998. "Predictors, Causes, and Correlates of Male Youth Violence." Pp. 421-75 in *Crime and Justice: A Review of Research v. 24*, edited by Michael Tonry and Mark H. Moore. Chicago: Chicago University Press.

_____. 2000. "Explaining and Preventing Crime: The Globalization of Knowledge—The American Society of Criminology 1999 Presidential Address." *Criminology* 38(1):1-24.

Farrington, David P., Leonard Berkowitz, and Donald J. West. 1982. "Differences between Individual and Group Fights." *British Journal of Social Psychology* 21:323-33.

Felson, Richard B. 1978. "Aggression as Impression Management." *Social Psychology* 41(3):205-13.

_____. 1981. "An Interactionist Approach to Aggression." Pp. 181-99 in *Impression Management Theory and Social Psychological Research*, edited by James T. Tedeschi. New York: Academic Press.

_____. 1982. "Impression Management and the Escalation of Aggression and Violence." *Social Psychology Quarterly* 45(4):245-54.

_____. 1984. "Patterns of Aggressive Social Interaction." Pp. 107-26 in *Social Psychology of Aggression: From Individual Behavior to Social Interaction*, edited by Amelie Mummendey. New York: Springer-Verlag.

_____. 1993. "Predatory and Dispute-Related Violence: A Social Interactionist Approach." Pp. 103-25 in *Routine Activity and Rational Choice: Advances in Criminological Theory*, edited by Ronald V. Clarke and Marcus Felson. New Brunswick: Transaction Publishers.

Felson, Richard B. and Henry J. Steadman. 1983. "Situational Factors in Disputes Leading to Criminal Violence." *Criminology* 21(1):59-74.

Felson, Richard B. and James T. Tedeschi. 1993. "Social Interactionist Perspectives on Aggression and Violence: An Introduction." Pp. 1-10 in *Aggression and Violence: Social Interactionist Perspectives*, edited by Richard B. Felson and James T. Tedeschi. Washington, D.C.: American Psychological Association.

Felson, Richard B. and Steven F. Messner. 1996. "To Kill or Not to Kill? Lethal Outcomes in Injurious Attacks." *Criminology* 34(4):519-45.

Felson, Richard B., Stephen A. Ribner, and Merryl S. Siegel. 1984. "Age and the Effect of Third Parties during Criminal Violence." *Sociology and Social Research* 68:452-62.

Felson, Richard B., Steven F. Messner, and Anthony Hoskin. 1999. "The Victim-Offender Relationship and Calling the Police in Assaults." *Criminology* 37(4):931-48.

Felson, Richard B., William Baccaglini, and George Gmelch. 1986. "Bar-Room Brawls: Aggression and Violence in Irish and American Bars." Pp. 153-66 in *Violent Transactions: The Limits of Personality*, edited by Anne Campbell and John J. Gibbs. Oxford: Basil Blackwell.

Felstiner, William L.F., Richard L. Abel, and Austin Sarat. 1980-81. "The Emergence and Transformation of Disputes: Naming, Blaming, Claiming..." *Law and Society Review* 15(3-4):631-54.

Gibbons, Don C. 1971. "Observations on the Study of Crime Causation." *American Journal of Sociology* 77(2):262-78.

Gibbs, John J. 1986. "Alcohol Consumption, Cognition and Context: Examining Tavern Violence." Pp. 133-51 in *Violent Transactions: The Limits of Personality*, edited by Anne Campbell and John J. Gibbs. Oxford: Basil Blackwell.

Giordano, Peggy C. 1978. "Girls, Guys and Gangs: The Changing Social Context of Female Delinquency." *Journal of Criminal Law and Criminology* 69:126-32.

Goffman, Erving. 1955. "On Face-Work: An Analysis of Ritual Elements in Social Interaction." *Psychiatry* 18:213-31.

_____. 1959. *The Presentation of Self in Everyday Life*. Garden City, NY: Anchor Books.

_____. 1967. *Interaction Ritual: Essays on Face-to Face Behavior*. Garden City, NY: Doubleday.

Goldstein, Paul J. 1989. "Drugs and Violent Crime." Pp. 16-48 in *Pathways to Criminal Violence*, edited by Neil Alan Weiner and Marvin E. Wolfgang. Newbury Park, CA: Sage Publications.

Goode, William. 1969. "Violence among Intimates." Pp. 941-77 in *Crimes of Violence: A Staff Report Submitted to the National Commission on the Causes and Prevention of Violence*, edited by Donald J. Mulvihill and Melvin M. Tumin. Washington, D.C.: U.S. Government Printing Office.

Gottfredson, Gary D. 1989. "The Experiences of Violent and Serious Victimization." Pp. 202-34 in *Pathways to Criminal Violence*, edited by Neil Alan Weiner and Marvin E. Wolfgang. Newbury Park: Sage Publications.

Gould, Roger V. 2003. *Collision of Wills: How Ambiguity about Social Rank Breeds Conflict.* Chicago: University of Chicago Press.

Greenberg, Stephanie W. 1981. "Alcohol and Crime: A Methodological Critique of the Literature." Pp. 70-109 in *Drinking and Crime: Perspectives on the Relationship between Alcohol Consumption and Criminal Behavior,* edited by James J. Collins, Jr. New York: The Guilford Press.

Halleck, Seymour L. 1975. "A Multi-Dimensional Approach to Violence." Pp. 33-47 in *Violence and Criminal Justice,* edited by Duncan Chappell and John Monahan. Lexington, MA: Lexington Books.

Hepburn, John R. 1973. "Violent Behavior in Interpersonal Relationships." *Sociological Quarterly* 14:419-29.

Hochstetler, Andy. 2001. "Opportunities and Decisions: Interactional Dynamics in Robbery and Burglary Groups." *Criminology* 39(3):737-64.

Horowitz, Ruth and Gary Schwartz. 1974. "Honor, Normative Ambiguity and Gang Violence." *American Sociological Review* 39:238-51.

Huff, C. Ronald (Ed.). 2002. *Gangs in America* (3rd ed.). Thousand Oaks, CA: Sage Publications.

Hughes, Lorine A. 2005. "Studying Youth Gangs: Alternative Methods and Conclusions." *Journal of Contemporary Criminal Justice* 21(2):98-119.
_____. Forthcoming. "Studying Youth Gangs: The Importance of Context." In Studying Youth Gangs, edited by James F. Short, Jr. and Lorine A. Hughes. Lanham, MD: AltaMira Press.

Hughes, Lorine A. and James F. Short, Jr. 2005. "Disputes Involving Youth Street Gang Members: Micro-social Contexts." *Criminology* 43(1):43-76.

Jankowski, Martin Sanchez. 1991. *Islands in the Street: Gangs and American Urban Society.* Berkeley, CA: University of California Press.

Jansyn, Leon R., Jr. 1966. "Solidarity and Delinquency in a Street Corner Group." *American Sociological Review* 31:600-14.

Katz, Jack. 1988. *The Seductions of Crime: Moral and Sensual Attractions in Doing Evil.* New York: Basic Books.

Kleck, Gary and Karen McElrath. 1991. "The Effects of Weaponry on Human Violence." *Social Forces* 69(3):669-92.

Klein, Malcolm M. 1971. *Street Gangs and Street Workers.* Englewood Cliffs, NJ: Prentice-Hall.
_____. 1995. *The American Street Gang: Its Nature, Prevalence, and Control.* New York: Oxford University Press.

Klein, Malcolm W. and Lois Y. Crawford. 1967. "Groups, Gangs, and Cohesiveness." *Journal of Research in Crime and Delinquency* 4:63-75.

Klein, Malcolm W., Cheryl L. Maxson, and Jody Miller (Eds.). 1995. *The Modern Gang Reader*. Los Angeles: Roxbury.

Kubrin, Charis E. and Ronald Weitzer. 2003. "Retaliatory Homicide: Concentrated Disadvantage and Neighborhood Culture." *Social Problems* 50: 157-80.

LaFree, Gary and Christopher Birbeck. 1991. "The Neglected Situation: A Cross-National Study of the Situational Characteristics of Crime." *Criminology* 29(1):73-98.

Levinson, David. 1983a. "Alcohol Use and Aggression in American Subcultures." Pp. 306-21 in *Alcohol and Disinhibition: Nature and Meaning of the Link*, edited by Robin Room and Gary Collins. Rockville, MD: National Institute on Alcohol Abuse and Alcoholism.

_____. 1983b. "Social Setting, Cultural Factors and Alcohol-Related Aggression." Pp. 41-58 in *Alcohol, Drug Abuse and Aggression*, edited by Keith A. Druley Edward Gottheil, Thomas E. Skoloda. Springfield, IL: Charles C. Thomas.

Loftin, Colin, Karen Kindley, Sandra L. Norris, and Brian Wiersema. 1987. "An Attribute Approach to Relationships between Offenders and Victims in Homicide." *Journal of Criminal Law and Criminology* 78(2):259-71.

Luckenbill, David F. 1977. "Criminal Homicide as a Situated Transaction." *Social Problems* 25:176-86.

_____. 1980. "Patterns of Force in Robbery." *Deviant Behavior* 1:361-78.

Luckenbill, David F. and Daniel P. Doyle. 1989. "Structural Position and Violence: Developing a Cultural Explanation." *Criminology* 27(3):419-36.

Lucore, Patricia. 1975. "Cohesiveness in the Gang." Pp. 92-110 in *Gang Delinquency*, edited by Desmond S. Cartwright, Barbara Tomson, and Hershey Schwartz. Monterey, CA: Brooks/Cole Publishing.

MacAndrew, Craig and Robert B. Edgerton. 1969. *Drunken Comportment: A Social Explanation*. Chicago: Aldine Publishing.

McIntyre, Lisa J. 1999. *The Practical Skeptic: Core Concepts in Sociology*. Mountain View, CA: Mayfield.

Mendelsohn, B. 1963. "The Origin of the Doctrine of Victimology." *Excerpta Criminological* 3:239-44.

Miethe, Terance D. and Robert F. Meier. 1994. *Crime and Its Social Context: Toward an Integrated Theory of Offenders, Victims, and Situations*. New York: State University of New York Press.

Miller, Walter B. 1958. "Lower Class Culture as a Generating Milieu of Gang Delinquency." *Journal of Social Issues* 14:5-19.

Miller, Walter B., Hildred Geertz, and Henry S.G. Cutter. 1961. "Aggression in a Boys' Street-Corner Group." *Psychiatry* 24:283-298.

Monahan, John. 1975. "The Prediction of Violence." Pp. 15-31 in *Violence and Criminal Justice*, edited by Duncan Chappell and John Monahan. Lexington, MA: Lexington Books.

Monahan, John and Deidre Klassen. 1982. "Situational Approaches to Understanding and Predicting Individual Violent Behavior." Pp. 292-319 in *Criminal Violence*, edited by Marvin E. Wolfgang and Neil Alan Weiner. Beverly Hills, CA: Sage Publications.

Morash, Merry. 1983. "Gangs, Groups, and Delinquency." *British Journal of Criminology* 23(4):309-35.

Mullins, Christopher W., Richard Wright, and Bruce A. Jacobs. 2004. "Gender, Streetlife, and Criminal Retaliation." *Criminology* 41:911-940.

Mummendey, Amelie and Sabine Otten. 1993. "Aggression: Interaction between Individuals and Social Groups." Pp. 145-67 in *Aggression and Violence: Social Interactionist Perspectives*, edited by Richard B. Felson and James T. Tedeschi. Washington, D.C.: American Psychological Association.

Oliver, William. 1994. *The Violent Social World of Black Men*. New York: Lexington Books.

Parker, Robert Nash. 1993. "The Effect of Context on Alcohol and Violence." *Alcohol Health and Research World* 17:117-22.

Parker, Robert Nash (with Linda-Anne Rebuhum). 1995. *Alcohol and Homicide: A Deadly Combination of Two American Traditions*. Albany, NY: SUNY Press.

Pecar, Janez. 1972. "Involved Bystanders: Examination of a Neglected Aspect of Criminology and Victimology." *International Journal of Contemporary Sociology* 9(2-3):81-87.

Pernanen, Kai. 1981. "Theoretical Aspects of the Relationship between Alcohol Use and Crime." Pp. 1-69 in *Drinking and Crime: Perspectives on the Relationship between Alcohol Consumption and Criminal Behavior*, edited by James J. Collins, Jr. New York: The Guilford Press.

_____. 1991. *Alcohol in Human Violence*. New York: The Guilford Press.

Pervin, Lawrence A. 1976. "A Free-Response Description Approach to the Analysis of Person-Situation Interaction." *Journal of Personality and Social Psychology* 34(3):465-74.

_____. 1978. "Definitions, Measurements, and Classifications of Stimuli, Situations, and Environments." *Human Ecology* 6(1):71-105.

Pittman, David J. and William Handy. 1964. "Patterns in Criminal Aggravated Assault." *Journal of Criminal Law and Criminology* 55:462-70.

Pokorny, Alex D. 1965. "Human Violence: A Comparison of Homicide, Aggravated Assault, Suicide, and Attempted Suicide." *Journal of Criminal Law and Criminology* 56(4):488-97.

Pruitt, Dean G. and Douglas F. Johnson. 1970. "Mediation as an Aid to Face Saving in Negotiation." *Journal of Personality and Social Psychology* 14(3):239-46.

Reiss, Albert J., Jr. and Jeffrey A. Roth (Eds.). 1993. *Understanding and Preventing Violence*. Panel on the Understanding and Control of Violent Behavior, Committee on Law and Justice, Commission on Behavioral and Social Sciences and Education, National Research Council. Washington, D.C.: National Academy Press.

Rhodes, Richard. 1999. *Why They Kill: The Discoveries of a Maverick Criminologist*. New York: Vintage Books.

Richardson, Deborah Capasso, Sandy Bernstein, and Stuart P. Taylor. 1979. "The Effect of Situational Contingencies on Female Retaliative Behavior." *Journal of Personality and Social Psychology* 37(11):2044-48.

Roman, Paul M. 1981. "Situational Factors in the Relationship between Alcohol and Crime." Pp. 143-51 in *Drinking and Crime: Perspectives on the Relationship between Alcohol Consumption and Criminal Behavior*, edited by James J. Collins, Jr. New York: The Guilford Press.

Roncek, Dennis W. and Pamela A. Maier. 1991. "Bars, Blocks, and Crimes Revisited: Linking the Theory of Routine Activities to the Empiricism of 'Hot Spots'" *Criminology* 29(4):725-53.

Rubin, Jeffrey Z. 1980. "Experimental Research on Third-Party Intervention in Conflict: Toward Some Generalizations." *Psychological Bulletin* 87(2):379-91.

Sampson, Robert J. and Janet L. Lauritsen. 1994. "Violent Victimization and Offending: Individual-, Situational-, and Community-Level Risk Factors." Pp. 1-114 in *Understanding and Preventing Violence*, edited by Albert J. Reiss and Jeffrey A. Roth. Washington, D.C.: National Academy Press.

Savitz, Leonard D., Korni Swaroop Kumar, and Margaret A. Zahn. 1991. "Quantifying Luckenbill." *Deviant Behavior* 12:19-19.

Schafer, Stephen. 1968. *The Victim and His Criminal: A Study in Functional Responsibility*. New York: Random House.

Schwartz, Gary. 1987. *Beyond Conformity or Rebellion: Youth and Authority in American*. Chicago: The University of Chicago Press.

Scott, Marvin B. and Stanford M. Lyman. 1968. "Accounts." *American Sociological Review* 33:46-62.

Shoham, Shlomo. 1972. "Points of No Return: Some Situational Aspects of Violence." Pp. 86-91 in *The Emotional Stress of War, Violence, and Peace*, edited by Rolland S. Parker. Pittsburgh: Stanwix House, Inc.

Shoham, Shlomo, Sara Ben-David, Rivka Vadmani, Joseph Atar, and Suzanne Fleming. 1973. "The Cycles of Interaction in Violence." Pp. 69-87 in *Israel Studies in Criminology*, edited by Shlomo Shoham. Jerusalem, Israel: Jerusalem Academic Press.

Short, James F., Jr. 1965. "Social Structure and Group Processes in Explanation of Gang Delinquency." Pp. 155-88 in *Problems of Youth: Transition to Adulthood in a Changing World*, edited by Muzafer Sherif and Carolyn W. Sherif. Chicago: Aldine Publishing.

_____. 1968. "Group Process, Cohesiveness, and Delinquency." Pp. 244-45 in *Gang Delinquency and Delinquent Subcultures*, edited by James F. Short, Jr. New York: Harper and Row.

_____. 1974. "Youth, Gangs and Society: Micro- and Macrosociological Processes." *Sociological Quarterly* 15:3-19.

_____. 1985. "The Level of Explanation Problem in Criminology." Pp. 51-72 in *Theoretical Methods in Criminology*, edited by Robert F. Meier. Beverly Hills, CA: Sage Publications.

_____. 1989. "Exploring Integration of Theoretical Levels of Explanation: Notes on Gang Delinquency." Pp. 243-59 in *Theoretical Integration in the Study of Deviance and Crime: Problems and Prospects*, edited by Marvin D. Krohn Steven F. Messner, and Allen E. Liska. New York: State University of New York.

_____. 1997. *Poverty, Ethnicity, and Violent Crime*. Boulder, CO: Westview.

_____. 1998. "The Level of Explanation Problem Revisited—The American Society of Criminology 1997 Presidential Address." *Criminology* 36(1):3-36.

_____. 2002. Personal Communication. Pullman, WA, December 11.

Short, James F., Jr. and Lorine A. Hughes (Eds.). Forthcoming. *Studying Youth Gangs*. Lanham, MD: AltaMira Pres.

Short, James F., Jr., Ramon Rivera, and Harvey Marshall. 1964. "Adult-Adolescent Relations and Gang Delinquency." *Pacific Sociological Review* 7(2):59-65.

Short, James F., Jr. and Fred L. Strodtbeck. 1965. *Group Process and Gang Delinquency*. Chicago: University of Chicago Press.

_____. 1968. "Why Gangs Fight." Pp. 246-255 in *Gang Delinquency and Delinquent Subcultures*, edited by James F. Short, Jr. New York: Harper and Row.

Silverman, David. 2001. *Interpreting Qualitative Data: Methods for Analysing Talk, Text and Interaction.* 2nd ed. London: Sage Publications.

Silverman, Linda J., Alba N. Rivera, and James T. Tedeschi. 1979. "Transgression-Compliance: Guilt, Negative Affect, or Impression Management." *Journal of Social Psychology* 108(1):57-62.

Silverman, Robert A. 1975. "Victim-Offender Relationships in Face-To-Face Delinquent Acts." *Social Problems* 22:383-93.

Silverman, Robert A. and Leslie W. Kennedy. 1987. "Relational Distance and Homicide: The Role of the Stranger." *Journal of Criminal Law and Criminology* 78(2):272-308.

Skogan, Wesley G. 1978. "Weapon Use in Robbery." Pp. 61-73 in *Violent Crime: Historical and Contemporary Issues*, edited by James A. Inciardi and Anne E. Pottieger. Beverly Hills: Sage Publications.

Sommers, Ira and Deborah R. Baskin. 1993. "The Situational Context of Violent Female Offending." *Journal of Research in Crime and Delinquency* 30(2):136-62.

Sparks, Richard F. 1982. *Research on Victims of Crime: Accomplishments, Issues, and New Directions.* Rockville, MD: Department of Health and Human Service.

Spergel, Irving A. 1995. *The Youth Gang Problem.* New York: Oxford University Press.

SPSS for Windows, Rel. 11.0.1. 2001. Chicago: SPSS Inc.

Steadman, Henry J. 1982. "A Situational Approach to Violence." *International Journal of Law and Psychiatry* 5(2):171-86.

Stokes, Randall and John P. Hewitt. 1976. "Aligning Actions." *American Sociological Review* 41:838-49.

Strodtbeck, Fred L. and James F. Short, Jr. 1964. "Aleatory Risks Versus Short-Run Hedonism in Explanation of Gang Action." *Social Problems* 12:127-40.

Sutherland, Edwin H. 1947. *Principles of Criminology.* Chicago: Lippincott.

Tannenbaum, Frank. 1938. *Crime and the Community.* New York: Ginn and Company.

Taylor, Minna and Eugene A. Weinstein. 1974. "Criticism, Witnesses and the Maintenance of Interaction." *Social Forces* 52:473-80.

Taylor, Stuart P. and Richard Pisano. 1971. "Physical Aggression as a Function of Frustration and Physical Attack." *Journal of Social Psychology* 84:261-67.

Tedeschi, James T. and Catherine A. Riordan. 1981. "Impression Management and Prosocial Behavior Following Transgression." Pp. 223-44 in *Impression Management Theory and Social Psychological Research*, edited by James T. Tedeschi. New York: Academic Press.

Tedeschi, James T. and Mitchell S. Nesler. 1993. "Grievances: Development and Reactions." Pp. 13-45 in *Aggression and Violence: Social Interactionist Perspectives*, edited by Richard B. Felson and James T. Tedeschi. Washington, D.C.: American Psychological Association.

Tedeschi, James T. and Paul Rosenfeld. 1981. "Impression Management Theory and the Forced Compliance Situation." Pp. 147-77 in *Impression Management Theory and Social Psychological Research*, edited by James T. Tedeschi. New York: Academic Press.

Tedeschi, James T., R. Bob Smith, III, and Robert C. Brown, Jr. 1974. "A Reinterpretation of Research on Aggression." *Psychological Bulletin* 81(9):540-62.

Thornberry, Terence P., Marvin D. Krohn, Alan J. Lizotte, and Deborah Chard-Wierschem. 1993. "The Role of Juvenile Gangs in Facilitating Delinquent Behavior." *Journal of Research in Crime and Delinquency* 30(1):55-87.

Thornberry, Terence P., Marvin D. Krohn, Alan J. Lizotte, Carolyn A. Smith, and Kimberly Tobin. 2003. *Gangs and Delinquency in Developmental Perspective*. Cambridge, UK: Cambridge University Press.

Thrasher, Frederic M. 1963. *The Gang: A Study of 1,313 Gangs in Chicago.* (Abridged ed.). Chicago: University of Chicago Press.

Tittle, Charles R. 1995. *Control Balance: Toward a General Theory of Deviance*. Boulder, CO: Westview.

Tittle, Charles R. and Raymond Paternoster. 2000. *Social Deviance and Crime: An Organizational and Theoretical Approach*. Los Angeles, CA: Roxbury.

Toch, Hans. 1969. *Violent Men: An Inquiry into the Psychology of Violence*. Chicago: Aldine Publishing.

Vigil, James Diego. 1988. *Barrio Gangs: Street Life and Identity in Southern California*. Austin, TX: University of Texas Press.

von Hentig, Hans. 1940. "Remarks on the Interaction of Perpetrator and Victim." *Journal of the American Institute of Criminal Law and Criminology* 31:303-09.

_____. 1948. *The Criminal and His Victim: Studies in the Sociobiology of Crime*. New Haven: Yale University Press.

Wallace, Samuel E. 1965. "Patterns of Violence in San Juan." Pp. 43-48 in *Interdisciplinary Problems in Criminology: Papers of the American Society of Criminology, 1964*, edited by Walter C. Reckless and Charles L. Newman. Columbus, OH: Ohio State University.

Warr, Mark. 2002. Companions in Crime: The Social Aspects of Criminal Conduct. Cambridge, UK: Cambridge University Press.

Watters, John K., Craig Reinarman, and Jeffrey Fagan. 1985. "Causality, Context, and Contingency: Relationships between Drug Abuse and Delinquency." *Contemporary Drug Problems* 12:351-73.

Weinstein, Eugene A. and Paul Deutschberger. 1963. "Some Dimensions of Altercasting." *Social Psychology* 26:454-66.

Wells, William and Julie Horney. 2002. "Weapon Effects and Individual Intent to Do Harm: The Escalation of Violence." *Criminology* 40(2):265-296.

Whyte, William Foote. 1943. *Street Corner Society*. Chicago: University of Chicago Press.

Wilkinson, Deanna L. 1998. "The Social and Symbolic Construction of Violent Events among Inner City Adolescent Males." *DAI-A 59/04, p. 1344, October 1998.* Newark, NJ: Rutgers, The State University of New Jersey.

Wilkinson, Deanna L. 2003. *Guns, Violence, and Identity among African American and Latino Youth*. New York: LFB Scholarly Publishing.

Williams, Kirk R. and Robert L. Flewelling. 1988. "The Social Production of Criminal Homicide: A Comparative Study of Disaggregated Rates in American Cities." *American Sociological Review* 53:421-31.

Wolfgang, Marvin E. 1957. "Victim-Precipitated Criminal Homicide." *Journal of Criminal Law, Criminology, and Police Science* 48(1):1-11.

_____. 1958. *Patterns in Criminal Homicide*. Philadelphia: University of Philadelphia.

Appendix A

CODING SCHEME
- *ID#*

- *Brief Verbal Description of Overall Context of Report*

- *Report Status*
  - 0   =   No potential incident
  - 1   =   Avoided Dispute-Related (Person) Incident
  - 2   =   Avoided Dispute-Related (Property) Incident
  - 3   =   Potential Dispute-Related (Person) Incident
  - 4   =   Potential Dispute-Related (Property) Incident
  - 5   =   Actual Dispute-Related (Person) Incident (action undertaken)
  - 6   =   Actual Dispute-Related (Property) Incident (action undertaken)

- *Source of Information (closest takes precedence)*
  - 1   =   Direct Observation
  - 2   =   Informed by Participant(s)
  - 3   =   Informed by Non-Participant Observer(s)
  - 4   =   Informed by Non-Participant Non-Observer(s)
  - 77   =   Indeterminable

- *Verbal Description of Type of Avoided, Potential, or Actual Incident*

- *Reason for Occurrence (Indicate relevant actor and target)*
  1 = Rule- or Order-Violation → Social Control/Punishment
  2 = Challenges to Identity/Status
  3 = Jealousy/Competition Over Opposite Sex
  4 = Self-defense
  5 = Robbery
  6 = Drug Business Transactions
  7 = Revenge/Retaliation (past gripes)
  8 = Defense of Others
  9 = Rumors
  10 = Territory/Neighborhood Honor
  11 = Money/Debts
  12 = Unfair/Rough Play (e.g., sports, etc.)
  13 = Misunderstanding
  14 = Fun/Recreation
  15 = Racial Concerns
  16 = Coping (with personal problems, etc.)
  17 = General Troublemaking
  18 = Other (specify)
  77 = Indeterminable

- *Outcome of Dispute-Related Incidents*
  0 = Non-Violent
  1 = Violent

- *Reason for Failure of Potential Violence to Escalate into Actual Violence*
  1 = Chance
  2 = No Threat to Reputation
  3 = Mediation
  4 = Peer Backup
  5 = No Peer Backup
  6 = Fear of Failing
  7 = Fear of Damaging Social Relationship
  8 = Deference
  9 = Legal Cost
  10 = Physical Cost (safety)
  11 = No Opportunity
  12 = Alternative Motivation
  13 = Realize Familiarity with Opposing Party

14 = Other (specify in next column)
77 = Indeterminable
99 = Not Applicable (Violence)

- *Date of Incident*
  ######## (Month, Day, Year)
  77 = Indeterminable

- *Location of Incident*
  0 = Private (Residence with no open party, Car, Clubroom, etc.)
  1 = Public (Bowling Alley, Pool Hall, Street/Street Corner, etc.)
  77 = Indeterminable

- *Territory*
  0 = Neither Offender nor Victim Territory
  1 = Offender Territory or Victim Territory
  2 = Both Offender and Victim Territory
  77 = Indeterminable

- *Total Number of People Present*
  Specify if given
  77 = Indeterminable

- *Total Number of People Involved in Incident*
  0 = 0
  1 = 1
  2 = 2 to 5
  3 = 6 or More
  77 = Indeterminable

- *Total Number of Gangs Present (gang or on behalf of gang)*
  Specify if given
  77 = Indeterminable

- *Total Number of Gangs Involved in Incident*
  Specify if given
  77 = Indeterminable

- *Offender Gang Membership*
  0 = No
  1 = Yes
  77 = Indeterminable

- *Offender Gang Identification*
  Specify
  77 = Indeterminable

- *Victim Gang Membership*
  0 = No
  1 = Yes
  77 = Indeterminable

- *Victim Gang Identification*
  Specify
  77 = Indeterminable

- *Relation of Victim to Offender*
  1 = Relative
  2 = Girlfriend/Boyfriend
  3 = Gang Member Friend
  4 = Non-gang Member Friend
  5 = Sponsored Gang Member
  6 = Detached Worker/Observer
  7 = Other Authority Figure
  8 = Rival
  9 = Acquaintance
  10 = Stranger
  11 = Other
  77 = Indeterminable

- *Offender-Victim Gang Relation*
  1 = Intra-gang
  2 = Inter-gang
  3 = Extra-group
  77 = Indeterminable
  99 = No gang relationship

- *Victim Present*
  - 0   =   No
  - 1   =   Yes
  - 77   =   Indeterminable

- *Detached Worker Present*
  - 0   =   No
  - 1   =   Yes
  - 77   =   Indeterminable

- *General Behavior of Detached Worker*
  - 0   =   Instigating
  - 1   =   Bystanding
  - 2   =   Mediating or Protecting
  - 3   =   Participating (i.e., as offender, victim, co-offender or co-victim)
  - 77   =   Indeterminable
  - 99   =   Not Applicable (not present or indeterminable)

- *Observer Present*
  - 0   =   No
  - 1   =   Yes
  - 77   =   Indeterminable

- *General Behavior of Observer*
  - 0   =   Instigating
  - 1   =   Bystanding
  - 2   =   Mediating or Protecting
  - 3   =   Participating (i.e., as offender, victim, co-offender or co-victim)
  - 77   =   Indeterminable
  - 99   =   Not Applicable (not present or indeterminable)

- *Presence of Third Party Other Than Detached Worker or Observer*
  - 0   =   No
  - 1   =   Yes
  - 77   =   Indeterminable

- *Third Party Gang Membership*
  - 0 = No
  - 1 = Yes (if at least one)
  - 77 = Indeterminable
  - 99 = Not Applicable (not present or indeterminable)

- *General Behavior of Third Party (code for acting third party; if none present or obvious, code for majority)*
  - 0 = Instigating
  - 1 = Bystanding
  - 2 = Mediating or Protecting
  - 77 = Indeterminable
  - 99 = Not Applicable (not present or indeterminable)

- *Characteristics of Primary Third Party*
  - 0 = Adult
  - 1 = Male Youth
  - 2 = Female Youth
  - 3 = Male and Female Youth
  - 4 = Other
  - 77 = Indeterminable
  - 99 = Not Applicable (not present or indeterminable)

(Begin: Include Detached Worker/Observer as Third Party)

- *Presence of Co-Offender(s)*
  - 0 = No
  - 1 = Yes
  - 77 = Indeterminable

- *Presence of Co-Victim(s)*
  - 0 = No
  - 1 = Yes
  - 77 = Indeterminable

- *Behavior of Co-Offender(s) Toward Offender*
  - 0 =   No Instigating Co-offenders
  - 1 =   Instigating Co-offenders
  - 77 = Indeterminable
  - 99 = Not Applicable (not present or indeterminable)

- *Behavior of Co-Victim(s) Toward Victim*
  - 0 =   No Instigating Co-victims
  - 1 =   Instigating Co-victims
  - 77 = Indeterminable
  - 99 = Not Applicable (not present or indeterminable)

- *Use of Intoxicants*
  - 0 =   Neither Party
  - 1 =   One Party
  - 2 =   Two Parties
  - 77 = Indeterminable

- *Possession of Weapons*
  - 0 =   Neither Party
  - 1 =   One Party
  - 2 =   Two Parties
  - 77 = Indeterminable

- *Threatened Use of Weapons*
  - 0 =   Neither Party
  - 1 =   One Party
  - 2 =   Two Parties
  - 77 = Indeterminable

- *Actual Use of Weapons*
  - 0 =   Neither Party
  - 1 =   One Party
  - 2 =   Two Parties
  - 77 = Indeterminable

- *Precedent for Offense*
  - 0 = No
  - 1 = Yes
  - 77 = Indeterminable

- *Types of Action*
  - 1 = Rule-violation
  - 2 = Reproach
  - 3 = Influence Attempt/Order
  - 4 = Compliance
  - 5 = Rebellious compliance
  - 6 = Non-compliance
  - 7 = Identity attack
  - 8 = Non-weapon Threat
  - 9 = Weapon Threat
  - 10 = Evasive Action
  - 11 = Mediation
  - 12 = Instigation
  - 13 = Account/Aligning Action
  - 14 = Physical Attack
  - 15 = Submission/Withdrawal

- *Actor/Target*
  - 1 = Offender
  - 2 = Victim
  - 3 = Third Party
  - 4 = Co-offender(s)
  - 5 = Co-victim(s)
  - 6 = Co-offender(s) and Co-victim(s)
  - 7 = Offender and Victim
  - 8 = Offender and Co-offender(s)
  - 9 = Victim and Co-victim(s)
  - 10 = All

- *Account or Aligning Action Offered by Offender*
  - 0 = No
  - 1 = Yes
  - 77 = Indeterminable
  - 99 = Not Applicable

- *Account or Aligning Action Offered by Victim*
  - 0 = No
  - 1 = Yes
  - 77 = Indeterminable
  - 99 = Not Applicable

- *Initial Norm-Violation, Non-compliance, Identity Attack*
  - 0 = No
  - 1 = Victim Norm-Violation
  - 2 = Victim Non-Compliance
  - 3 = Offender Identity Attack
  - 77 = Indeterminable

- *Apparent Seriousness of Incident*
  - 0 = No (horseplay, etc.)
  - 1 = Yes
  - 77 = Indeterminable

- *Offender Same Race as Victim*
  - 0 = No
  - 1 = Yes
  - 77 = Indeterminable

- *Mediation Before or After Violence*
  - 0 = Before
  - 1 = After
  - 77 = Indeterminable
  - 99 = Not applicable (no mediation)

- *Victim Resistance After Initial Attack by Offender*
  - 0 = No
  - 1 = Yes
  - 2 = Victim Attacks First
  - 77 = Indeterminable

- *Weapon Threat Before or After Violence*
  - 0   =   Before
  - 1   =   After
  - 77   =   Indeterminable
  - 99   =   Not Applicable (no weapons threat)

Appendix B

GANG, DETACHED WORKER, AND OBSERVER IDENTIFICATION

Gang	Worker	Observer
Comanche	C. Brown	
Egyptian Cobras	L. Dillard	
	G. Dryden	F. Cherry, L. Landry, B. Wright
Englewood Cobras	B. Gilmore	
Junior Imperials	E. Mitchell	B. Wright
M. Imperial Chaplains	C. Brown	J. Moland
	F. Hubbard	L. Landry
	P. McGuire	F. Cherry
	J. Morita	
Midget Vampires/Braves	E. Mitchell	J. Moland
Nobles	B. Gilmore	
	F. Hubbard	
	M. Riley	L. Landry, J. Moland
	B. Ross	F. Cherry, J. Moland, W. Pope, B. Wright

Black

Gang	Worker	Observer
North Side Vice Lords	J. Oldham	L. Landry, J. Moland
Vice Lords		
Senior	B. Gilmore	L. Landry, J. Moland
Junior	G. Dryden	L. Fishman, L. Landry, J. Moland
	L. Walker	
Midget	L. Walker	
South Side Cobras	M. Riley	
	B. Ross	L. Landry, J. Moland, B. Wright
	H. Young	J. Moland
Stateway Cobras	A. Smith	F. Cherry, J. Moland, B. Wright
Vagabonds	A. Smith	
Valiant Gents	B. Gilmore	L. Landry
	B. Ross	L. Landry, J. Moland
	H. Young	J. Moland
Vampires	E. Mitchell	L. Landry, J. Moland, B. Wright

Black

Gang	Detached Worker	Observer
80th and Halsted	G. Anderson	W. Pope
	L. Deering	J. Freedman, W. Pope
Clovers	B. Jemilo	J. Freedman
	G. Powell	W. Pope
Dukes/Lancers	J. Lamotte	J. Freedman, W. Pope
Gossage Grill	G. Anderson	W. Pope
Grand Crossing	J. Lamotte	
May Boys	G. Anderson	
	L. Deering	J. Freedman, W. Pope
Playboys	H. Bach	
	J. Morita	
Sub Grill	P. Gustofson	
	B. Jemilo	J. Freedman, W. Pope
	G. Powell	J. Freedman, W. Pope
Trios	B. Jemilo	J. Freedman, W. Pope
Wolf Park	J. Lamotte	
Wrightwood-Racine	B. Jemilo	
	G. Powell	

White

Index